George Washington Moon

The Dean's English

A criticism on the Dean of Canterbury's essays on the Queen's English. Tenth Edition

George Washington Moon

The Dean's English
A criticism on the Dean of Canterbury's essays on the Queen's English. Tenth Edition

ISBN/EAN: 9783337321901

Printed in Europe, USA, Canada, Australia, Japan

Cover: Foto ©ninafisch / pixelio.de

More available books at **www.hansebooks.com**

THE DEAN'S ENGLISH:

A Criticism on the Dean of Canterbury's Essays

ON THE

QUEEN'S ENGLISH.

BY

G. WASHINGTON MOON,

MEMBER OF THE COUNCIL
OF THE ROYAL SOCIETY OF LITERATURE,
AUTHOR OF
BAD ENGLISH EXPOSED, ETC.

Tenth Edition.

LONDON:
HATCHARDS, PICCADILLY.
1876.

"Literature, if it is to flourish, must have a standard of
"taste built up, which shall expand to meet new forms of
"excellence, but which shall preserve that which is excellent
"in old forms, and shall serve as a guide to the rejection
"of whatever is bad, pretentious, and artificial; and it is
"the business of critics to see that this standard is built up
"and maintained."—THE SATURDAY REVIEW.

PREFACE.

THE purity of the English language is as dear to educated Americans as it is to ourselves. One of them (A. J. C.) thus writes in a recent number of the New York 'ROUND TABLE':—

"The corrupter of a language stabs straight at the "heart of his country. He commits a crime against "every individual of the nation, for he throws a poison "into a stream from which all must drink. He wrongs "himself first, and afterward every man and woman "whose native speech he mars. It is the duty of every "educated man to guard zealously the purity of his "native tongue. No inheritance which can descend to an "individual or to a nation is comparable in value with a "language which possesses words into which may be "coined all great thoughts, pure motives, noble enter-"prises, grand endeavors, the wealth of philosophy, "poetry, and history, and even the beauty of the canvas "and the glory of the marble. He who does aught to "preserve such a language deserves the gratitude of his "people, as he who mars an organism so beautiful and "precious, merits their severest displeasure. He who "hunts down and pillories a slang phrase, a vulgarism, a "corruption of any kind, is a public benefactor. In the "fulfilment of the sacred trust which rests on him as an "educated man, he adds a stone to the bulwark of his "nation's safety and greatness."

My contribution towards that bulwark is this little work, which urges upon every Englishman the study of his own language, and points out to him the disgrace which he may incur by neglecting it. Incidentally the book cautions him against self-deception in this matter. It tells him of one who had received a collegiate education, had attained academical honours, was raised to the deanery of Canterbury, and who considered himself to be so unquestionably a master of the language, that he actually assumed the office of public lecturer on the Queen's English; and yet was so ignorant of its simplest rules, that the grossness of his errors in grammar and in composition, even in his lectures, made him the laughing-stock of those whom he thought himself competent to instruct.

But I wish it to be distinctly understood that in writing these criticisms I have not been actuated by any feeling of ill-will towards the Dean of Canterbury. I object not to the man, but to the man's language; it is extremely faulty; and since the faults of teachers, if suffered to pass uncondemned, soon become the teachers of faults, it was necessary that some one should take upon himself the task of "*demonstrating*", as 'THE 'EDINBURGH REVIEW' said, "*that while the Dean " undertook to instruct others, he was himself, but a " castaway in matters of grammar.*" As a Fellow of the Royal Society of Literature, one of the objects of which is "to preserve the purity of " the English language ", I took upon myself the demonstration. How far I have succeeded, each individual reader will determine for himself; but the yearly increasing sale of '*The Dean's English*' bears very flattering testimony to the fact that the work meets with the approval of the public generally. The best evidence, however, of its popularity is to be found in the circumstance that the book has been piratically reprinted in America *by the Dean's own publishers!* But, for the information of my Transatlantic readers, I mention that the American reprint is from an early issue of the work, and contains only a portion of the matter published in the subsequent editions.

As for the Dean's book, it certainly contains much valuable information, collected from various sources; but the information is blended with so very much that would be really injurious to the student of literature, that the work can never safely be recommended for his guidance. The style, too, in which it is written, is so hopelessly bad, that no alteration could obtain for it the praise of being a model for chasteness and elegance of expression. We read in it, of persons making "*a precious mess* of their work!" and expletives, we are informed, serve to "*grease the* "*wheels of talk*"! Some improvements, it is true, have been made in the second edition; *a man* is no longer spoken of by the slang phrase "*an "individual*"; but the Dean is so strangely forgetful of the courtesy due to women, that he uses, respecting them, the most debasing of all slang phrases. When speaking of even our Sovereign Lady, the Queen, he describes her by an epithet which is equally applicable to a dog! Her Majesty is a—"*female*"! We speak of "*dog-Latin*"; what more appropriate name than "*dog-English*" could be given to ungentlemanly language like this? and how could we better serve the interests of literature than by hooting all such "*dog-English*" out of society? "The power of sneering", says Professor Masson, "was given to man to be "used; and nothing is more gratifying than to "see an idea which is proving a nuisance, sent "clattering away with a hue and cry after it, "and a tin kettle tied to its tail."

The Dean has just published an appendix to his '*Queen's English*'. It was said that, if he should ever write again upon language, he would, doubtless, write with greater care. The reviewers were very charitable to attribute his errors to carelessness; but, that those errors sprang from an other source, is now evident beyond dispute:— the appendix, although written after four years' more study, abounds with errors as gross as any that were found in the Dean's first essay. What does the reader think of there being, in a treatise on the Queen's English, such an error in grammar as the following:—"'*Abnormal*' is one of those "words which has come in to supply a want in "the precise statements of science":—*those words which has come!* As for the courtesies of literature, the Dean calls those persons who differ with him in the use of certain words, "*apes*", "*asses*", and "*idiots*". Is this "sound speech, that cannot "be condemned": Titus ii, 8? Is this being "gentle unto all men, apt to teach, patient, in "meekness instructing those that oppose them-"selves": 2 Timothy ii, 24? But I forbear.

Surely, surely, it will be only modest of the Dean to retire from the office of lecturer on the Queen's English; and, if his good sense has not utterly left him, he will wisely reflect on the folly of attracting attention to a style of writing "*which*", as Junius said of the character of Sir William Draper, "*will only pass without censure when it passes without observation.*"

LONDON,
January, 1867.

The Very Rev. Henry Alford, D.D., Dean of Canterbury, was born in London on October 7th, 1810, and was the son of the Rev. Henry Alford, M.A., of Wadham College, Oxford, Vicar of Aston Sandford, near Thame, in Buckinghamshire (the living held by the Bible Commentator, Thomas Scott). Having received his early education in the Grammar School of Ilminster, in Somersetshire, he matriculated, in 1828, at Trinity College, Cambridge, of which Society he was soon afterwards elected a Scholar. In 1831 he obtained two University distinctions, being elected Bell's Scholar and Member's (Latin) Prizeman. In the following year he took the degree of B.A. in double first-class honours, being placed thirty-seventh in the list of Wranglers, and eighth in the first-class in the Classical Tripos. He further graduated M.A. 1835, B.D. 1849, and D.D. 1859. He was ordained Deacon in 1833, by Bishop Philpotts of Exeter, and Priest in 1834, by Bishop Murray of Rochester. His appointments and preferments were: 1833–35, Curate of Ampton, in the county of Suffolk; 1834–35, Fellow of Trinity; 1835–53, Vicar of Wymeswold, in the county of Leicester and diocese of Peterborough, a benefice in the patronage of his College; 1841–42, Hulsean Lecturer in the University of Cambridge; 1842 (for several years), Examiner in Logic and Moral Philosophy in the University of London; 1853–57, Minister of Quebec Chapel, in the parish of St. Marylebone; and from 1857 to his death Dean of Canterbury.

He died at Canterbury on January 12th, 1871.

CONTENTS.

ADJECTIVES.
	PAGE
"A *decided* weak point", or "A *decidedly* weak point"	48
"Not *a strict* neuter-substantive", or "Not *strictly a* neuter-substantive" . . . 50,	123
"Speak *no coarser* than usual", or "Speak *not more coarsely* than usual" . . . 49,	83
"The words *nearest* connected", or "The words *most nearly* connected"	49
The rule respecting "*first and last*" and "*former and latter*"	162
"Less" and "lesser"	186

ADVERBS.
Dr. Blair on adverbs	14
"Hath the Lord *only spoken* by Moses?", or "Hath the Lord spoken *only by Moses?*" . . 73, 87,	127
"His own use so *frequently* of it", or "His own so *frequent* use of it"	87
"How *nicely* she looks", or "How *nice* she looks" .	86
"It appears still more *plainly*", or "It appears still more *plain*"	86
"I *only bring forward* some things", or "I bring forward *some things only*" . . . 14,	118
"They may *be correctly* classified", or "They may *correctly be* classified" . . . 101,	128
"We *merely speak* of numbers", or "We speak of numbers *merely*"	14
"Rather familiar"	171

AMBIGUITY.

	PAGE
Dr. Campbell on constructive ambiguity	21
Lord Kames on constructive ambiguity	10
A backwood planted with thoughts	55
A man losing his mother in the papers	13, 118
A paragraph of fewer than ten lines, yet so ambiguously worded that it admits of 10,240 different readings	30, 61, 125
A strange sentence from Dean Swift's writings	16
A witness "intoxicated by the motion of an honourable member"	17
"Compositors without any mercy"	12
"Compositors without the slightest compunction"	11, 117
Defiling a detachment of soldiers	19
Disappointed ambition	19
Expressing a sentence, or expressing the meaning	58
Expressing a woman	58
Human kidneys in dogs	31
Intellectual qualities of raiment	32
Incongruous association of ideas	60
"I will introduce the body of—my essay"	12, 117
Literary Frenchmen	17, 119
Obscure writing	96
Professors walking off with dictionaries	56, 125
Solemn characters	171
"Sometimes the editors *fall, from their ignorance*"	9
"The beaux painted their faces, *as well as the women*"	17
"The Greeks wheeled about and halted, *with the river on their backs*"	19
"The one rule *of all others*"	49, 122

CONJUNCTIONS.

Does "than" govern the accusative case?	47, 85, 159, 165, 182
"As well as", and "So well as"	92
"*This* [as well as that] *fix* it"	104, 129
"Try *and* think", or "try *to* think"	166

CONTENTS.

ELLIPSIS.

	PAGE
Brevity should be subordinate to perspicuity	99
Unallowable ellipsis	25
"We call a cup-board a cubbard, *and so of* many other compound words"	53, 124

EMPHASIS.

The use of emphasis	24
The misuse of emphasis—"And they *did* eat"	25
"Saddle me the ass. And they saddled *him*"	80

FINE LANGUAGE.

"Call a spade *a spade*"	138
"Chrononhotonthologos"	138
A man is "*an individual*", or "*a person*", or "*a party*"	140, 144
A woman is "*a female*", or "*a lady*", or "*a young person*"	141
A bull is "*a gentleman cow*"	141
A bitch is "*a lady dog*"	141
Boys and girls are "*young gentlemen*", "*young ladies*", "*juveniles*", or "*juvenile members of society*"	142
To live in a house is "*to reside in a residence*"	142
An inn is "*an hotel*"	142
A room is "*an apartment*"	142
Lords and nobles are "*the aristocracy*"	142
The people of England are "*the million*", or "*the masses*"	143
To take a walk is "*to promenade*"	143
Landowners are "*proprietors*"	143
Farmers and yeoman are "*agriculturists*"	143
A working man is "*an operative*"	143
A place is "*a locality*"	143
A celebrated person is "*a celebrity*"	143
A maid-of-all-work speaks of her "*situation*"	143
A house-agent speaks of his "*clients*"	143

	PAGE
A schoolmaster is a "*Principal of a Collegiate Institution*"	143
To be buried is "*to be interred*"	143
A churchyard is "*a cemetery*" or "*a necropolis*"	143
To ask is "*to inquire*"	145
To speak of is "*to allude to*"	145

NOUNS.

Relatives without any nouns to which they refer	31, 121
Singular or plural	52

OBSCURITY. [See Ambiguity].

PERSPICUITY.

What is perspicuity?	22
The most essential quality in all writings	23
[See also Ambiguity].	

PREPOSITIONS.

"Different to", or "Different from"	48
Errors in the use of the preposition "*from*"	10, 91
"In respect of", or "With respect to"	58
Not "five *outs* and one *in*", but five *ins* and one *out*	107
"The cat jumped on [to] the chair"	38, 186
"Treating an exception", or "Treating *of* an exception"	58, 99

PRONOUNS.

Dr. Campbell on pronouns	29
A difficulty of *him*	56
A paragraph with twenty-eight nouns intervening between the pronoun and its noun	32, 61, 122
"As tall as *him*", "As tall as *me*"	161
"It is *I*", or "It is *me*"	48, 156, 172, 183
"It is *her*"	157, 184
Misuse of pronouns	29
"More than *I*", or "More than *me*"	85, 159

CONTENTS.   xxi

	PAGE
"Our Father which [or *who*] art in Heaven"	. 188
"Than *who*", or "Than *whom*"	. 160, 166, 209
"Than *he*"	166, 205
The test of a scholar's mastery over the language	. 28
The pronoun "*its*" occurs only once in the Bible	33, 122
The date of the introduction of "*its*" into the Bible	70, 126
The origin of "*its*"	. 179
"The nations not so blest as *thee*"	. 161
The relation between nouns and pronouns, the great stumbling-block to most writers	. 31
"This" and "that"	. 168
"Thou" and "thee", when used	6, 64, 117
William Cobbett on "*it*"	. 32
"*Which* I do"	. 167
Tom and Jack	. 174
"He'd a stick and he'd a stick"	. 174
"Between you and *I*"	. 206

PRONUNCIATION.

"Covetous", or "Covetious"	30, 62, 199
The pronunciation of Greek proper names	27, 66, 121, 199
Should the "*h*" in "*humble*" be aspirated?	27, 163, 188
American pronunciation of the aspirate "*h*"	48, 197
"Mănifold" and "Mănifest"	. 188
"When" and "wen"; "whet" and "wet"; "white" and "wight"; "wheel" and "weal"; "which" and "witch"; "whine" and "wine"	. 198
"Lawr", "idear", "Jehovahr", "peninsular"	. 198
"Doah", for door, "*pore*", for poor, "hoarse", for horse, &c.	. 198
The "*t*" not sounded in "apostle", "epistle", "often"	199

PUNCTUATION.

An error occasioned by the *insertion* of a comma	. 100
An error occasioned by the *misplacing* of a comma	. 103
An error occasioned by the *omission* of a comma,	11, 20 97, 117
Lord Kames on punctuation	. 10

SENTENCES.

	PAGE
Blair and Campbell on the construction of sentences	15, 16, 21
Lord Kames on the construction of sentences	10, 15
Other authorities on the construction of sentences	16
Examples of the violations of the law respecting the position of words in a sentence	17, 18, 19, 119, 120, 125, 172
Objectionable construction of sentences	59
"Squinting construction"	20, 100
The natural order of constructing a sentence	59

SLANG.

"A juvenile"	142
"A female"	102, 120, 141
"An individual"	59, 125, 140
"A party"	144, 169
"A tipple"	169
"A trap"	169
"Come to grief"	25, 120, 169

SPELLING.

"Honor", or "Honour"	29, 81, 184, 196
"Odor", or "Odour"	82
"Tenor", or "Tenour"	42
"Reliable", or "Rely-upon-able"	184
"Savior", or "Saviour"	196

TAUTOLOGY AND TAUTOPHANY.

"*Abated* the nuisance by enacting that the *debateable* syllable", &c.	106, 129
"*Account* for specimens, for which the author must not be *accounted* responsible"	106
"A *counter*-roll or check on the *accounts*. From this *account* of the word it appears", &c.	106
Five *ins* and one *out*	107
Three *ins* following each other,—"in in in"	24
Other, other, others	106

CONTENTS. xxiii

PAGE

VERBS.

"He *ate no* dinner" 175
"I ain't certain", "I ain't going" . . . 98
"I need not have troubled myself" . . . 54
"Stick no bills" 174
"The next point which I notice shall be", &c. . . 56
"There are three first and [there are] one last" 51, 123
The verb "to leave" 161
The verb "to progress" 57
"To the former belong three, to the latter [belong] one 51, 123
"Twice one *is* two", or "twice one *are* two" . . 54
"Would have been broken to pieces, or [would have been] come to grief" . . 25, 60, 120, 164

MISCELLANEOUS.

The power of example 3
Dr. Campbell on the formation of languages . . 3
The office of the grammarian and of the critic . 4
The influence of popular writers . . . 6
Throwing stones 6
Persuasive teaching 7
"*The Times*" . . . 7, 8, 9, 103, 104
"Mending their *ways*", "*highways*", "*by-roads*", and "*private roads*" . . . 11, 117
Great things which hang up framed at railway stations 18, 119
"Individuals in social intercourse" . . 18, 120
The source of mistakes . . . 26, 121
"Odious" and "odorous" 28
The language of the Bible . . 28, 89, 190, 209
"Be courteous" 34, 76
"We do not write for idiots" . . . 36
"A most abnormal elongation of the auricular appendages" 37, 74
Call a spade, *a spade* . . . 37, 138
Falling *up* into a *depth* 36
"No case, abuse the plaintiff" . . . 37

CONTENTS.

	PAGE
"Open up"	45
A language that grew *up* by being brought *down*	46
Neglect of the study of English at our public schools	47
"An individual occurring in Shakspeare"	59, 125
A fact "stated into prominence"	59
A bottomless swamp "filled in"	60
Eating and being "filled up"	60
Dean's English	61
A literary curiosity	63, 126
The play of Hamlet with the ghost left out	64
Misquotation of an opponent's words	65, 83
Strange errors in an old edition of the Scriptures	71
Misquotation of Scripture	73, 127, 178
"Why do you call me an ass?"	74
Explanation respecting the charge of discourtesy	76
A teacher is always amenable to criticism	80
What is a nucleus?	82
"No more" and "never again"	83
"Right to a *t*"	85
The importance of trifles	92
John Milton on rules and maxims	94, 212
An anecdote of Douglas Jerrold	96
"The *final* 'u' in tenour" and "the *final* 's' in months"	105
No special training in English at our colleges	47, 107, 193
The English language compared to a temple	112
The prospects of the English language	113, 192
Precept *v.* practice	115
"Punch the barber"	116
Parallelisms	131
"The Cat's paw"	148
The injurious effects of Dean Alford's essays	155
Dr. Alford's abuse of the Americans	177
Americanisms	195
Idioms	200
Methinks	202
"I'd", a contraction of "I had", and of "I would"	203

THE DEAN'S ENGLISH:

A CRITICISM.

To the Very Rev. Henry Alford, D.D., Dean of Canterbury.

Rev. Sir,

On the publication of your *'Plea for the Queen's 'English'* * I was surprised to observe inaccuracies in the structure of your sentences, and also more than one grammatical error. Under ordinary circumstances I should not have taken notice of such deviations from what is strictly correct in composition; but the subject of your essay being the Queen's English, my attention was naturally drawn to the language you had employed; and as, when I privately wrote to you respecting it, you justified

---

* '*A Plea for the Queen's English*', by the Dean of Canterbury: '*Good Words*', March, 1863.

your use of the expressions to which I had referred, I am desirous of knowing whether such expressions are really allowable in writings, and especially whether they are allowable in an essay which has for its object the exposure and correction of literary inaccuracies. I therefore *publish* this my second letter to you; and I do so, to draw forth criticism upon the rules involved in this question; that, the light of various opinions being made to converge upon these rules, their value or their worthlessness may thereby be manifested. I make no apology for this course; for when, by your violations of syntax and your defence of those violations, you teach that Campbell's '*Philosophy of Rhetoric*', Kames's '*Elements of Criticism*', and Blair's '*Lectures on Rhetoric and Belles Lettres*' are no longer to be our guides in the study of the English language, no apology is needed from me for my asking the public whether they confirm the opinion that these hitherto acknowledged authorities should be superseded.

To spread this inquiry widely is the more necessary, because, on account of the position which you hold, and the literary reputation which you enjoy, your modes of expression, if suffered to pass unchallenged, will, probably, by and by be quoted in justification of the style of other writers who shall presume to damage by example, if not by precept, the highway of thought over which all desire to travel.

By influential example it is that languages are moulded into whatever form they take; therefore, according as example is for good or for evil, so will a language gain in strength, sweetness, precision, and elegance, or will become weak, harsh, unmeaning, and barbarous. Popular writers may make or may mar a language. It is with them, and not with grammarians, that the responsibility rests; for language is what custom makes it; and custom is, has been, and always will be, more influenced by example than by precept.

Dr. Campbell, speaking of the formation of languages, justly says:—* "Language is purely a "species of fashion, in which, by the general, but "tacit, consent of the people of a particular state "or country, certain sounds come to be appropriated "to certain things as their signs, and certain ways "of inflecting and of combining those sounds come "to be established as denoting the relations which "subsist among the things signified. It is not the "business of grammar, as some critics seem pre-

* Campbell's *Philosophy of Rhetoric*, vol. i, book 2, chap. 1, 2.

"posterously to imagine, to give law to the fashions
"which regulate our speech. On the contrary,
"from its conformity to these, and from that alone,
"it derives all its authority and value. For, what
"is the grammar of any language? It is no other
"than a collection of general observations metho-
"dically digested, and comprising all the modes
"previously and independently established, by
"which the significations, derivations, and combi-
"nations of words in that language are ascertained.
"It is of no consequence here to what causes origi-
"nally these modes or fashions owe their existence
"—to imitation, to reflection, to affectation, or to
"caprice; they no sooner are accepted and become
"general than they are the laws of the language,
"and the grammarian's only business is to note,
"collect, and methodise them." "'But,' it may be
"said, 'if custom, which is so capricious and
"'unaccountable, is everything in language, of
"'what significance is either the grammarian or the
"'critic?' Of considerable significance notwith-
"standing; and of most then, when they confine
"themselves to their legal departments, and do not
"usurp an authority that does not belong to them.
"The man who, in a country like ours, should
"compile a succinct, perspicuous, and faithful digest

"of the laws, though no lawgiver, would be univer-
"sally acknowledged to be a public benefactor.
"How easy would that important branch of
"knowledge be rendered by such a work, in
"comparison with what it must be when we have
"nothing to have recourse to but a labyrinth of
"statutes, reports, and opinions. That man also
"would be of considerable use, though not in the
"same degree, who should vigilantly attend to every
"illegal practice that were beginning to prevail, and
"should evince its danger by exposing its contra-
"riety to law. Of similar benefit, though in a
"different sphere, are grammar and criticism. In
"language, the grammarian is properly the compiler
"of the digest; and the verbal critic, is the man who
"seasonably notifies the abuses that are creeping
"in. Both tend to facilitate the study of the
"tongue to strangers, to render natives more perfect
"in the knowledge of it, to advance general use
"into universal, and to give a greater stability at
"least, if not a permanency, to custom, that most
"mutable thing in nature."

I have quoted these passages because they have direct reference to the subject under consideration; for I do not find fault with the critical remarks in your essay. Many of them, it is true, are not new;

but most of them are good, and therefore will bear re-perusal; yet it was scarcely necessary to repeat in the March number of *'Good Words'*, the meaning of "*avocation*", which Archbishop Whately had given in the same magazine in the previous August; and so far from its being "so well known a fact" that we reserve the singular pronouns "thou" and "thee" "*entirely* for our addresses in prayer to "Him who is the highest Personality", it is not a fact. These pronouns are very extensively and very properly used in poetry, even when inanimate objects are addressed; as is the case in the following lines from Coleridge's '*Address to Mont 'Blanc'*:—

> "O dread and silent Mount! I gazed upon *thee*
> "Till *thou*, still present to the bodily sense,
> "Didst vanish from my thought: entranced in prayer
> "I worshipped the Invisible alone."

However, I shall not notice your critical remarks, for they are of only secondary importance. Very little can be added to the canons of criticism already laid down; very much may be done for the permanent enriching of our language, by popular writers' exercising more care as to the examples which they set in composition, than as to the lessons which they teach concerning it.

But in literature especially, it has always been so much easier for critics to censure than to guide by example; and it has been thought by them so much better fun to break an author's windows than to stay quietly at home taking care of their own, that the throwing of stones has long been a favourite amusement. Nor do we object to it, providing two things be granted: the one, that the glass of the windows is so bad that the objects seen through it appear distorted; the other, that in no spirit of unkindness shall the stones be thrown, lest the critic not only break the author's windows, but also wound the author himself.

It must be admitted that there is in your essay so little of the "sweetness of the lips" which "increaseth learning", that but a very small amount of good can accrue to those whom you think to be most in need of improvement. You speak of "*the vitiated and pretentious style which "passes current in our newspapers*". You sneeringly say, "*In a leading article of 'The Times' not long "since, was this beautiful piece of slipshod English :*" then follows the quotation, with this remark appended, "*Here we see faults enough besides the "wretched violations of grammar*"; and, "*these writers "are constantly doing something like this.*"

That the reader may be able to form some idea of the labour attendant upon one issue of our leading daily paper, of which you speak so contemptuously, I subjoin an extract from a work by Henry Mayhew:—

"The TIMES NEWSPAPER of March 25th, 1865, "is now before us. It consists of eighteen large "pages, each more than two feet long and one and "a half broad; so that the paper contains not fewer "than fifty-four square feet of printed matter. "Each of these eighteen pages consists of six "columns, and the whole 108, when pasted together "in one strip, would form a streamer very nearly "200 feet long; and as each column has, on an "average, as many as 226 lines, there are in round "numbers not fewer than 24,500 lines in the entire "body of the work; so that, estimating each line to "be made up of ten words, there must be nearly "a quarter of a million of such words throughout "the publication. Then, assuming each word to "consist, generally speaking, of six letters, we "arrive at the result that there are nearly *a million* "*and a half of types* which have to be picked up "and arranged in their places daily.

"Look at the print as closely as you will—scan "it as minutely as any professional printer's eyes

"would scrutinise it for errors of the press, and it
"will be difficult to find one letter turned upside-
"down—one mistake in spelling—one fault in
"punctuation—one slip in grammar, or even one
"inelegance in composition—throughout the entire
"mass. And yet all this wonderful extent of
"matter has been written, composed, and corrected,
"in one day and night."

A writer in '*The Glasgow Christian News*' says:
"When it is considered that in every newspaper of
"any pretensions there are articles, letters, and par-
"agraphs, from thirty or forty different pens, there
"is not much to be astonished at in occasional
"blunders. If the Dean knew more of newspaper
"matters he would be more charitable in his criti-
"cism. Is it fair to expect in a leading article
"composed at midnight, against time, and carried
"off to the printers, slip by slip as it is written, the
"same rhythmical beauty and accuracy of expres-
"sion as in any essay elaborated by the labour of
"many days for a quarterly review? Yet the
"English of the Dean, corrected and re-corrected,
"pales before that of '*The Times*' written perhaps
"by a wearied man at two in the morning."

You say, "*Sometimes the editors of our papers fall,
"from their ignorance, into absurd mistakes*". Cer-

tainly not a very happy arrangement of words in which to remark upon the "absurd mistakes" of other people; for we ought to be as careful what our sentences suggest, as what they affirm; and we are so accustomed to speak of people *falling from* a state or position, that your words naturally suggest the absurd idea of editors falling from their ignorance.

I submit it to the reviewers whether your sentence is not altogether faulty. The words, "from "their ignorance" should not come after "fall", they should precede it. But, for the reason just given, the word "from" is objectionable in any part of the sentence, which would have been better written thus, Sometimes our editors, in consequence of their ignorance, fall into absurd mistakes. If you say that the defect in perspicuity is removed by the punctuation, I answer, in the language of Lord Kames, "Punctuation may remove an ambi-"guity, but will never produce that peculiar beauty "which is perceived when the sense comes out "clearly and distinctly by means of a happy "arrangement". The same high authority tells us that a circumstance ought never to be placed between two capital members of a sentence; or if it be so placed, the first word in the consequent member should be one that cannot connect it with that which precedes. In your sentence, unfortunately, the connection is perfect, and the suggestion of a ridiculous idea is the result.

Nor is the foregoing the only instance of this kind of faulty arrangement. You say, "The great "enemies to understanding anything printed in "our language are the commas. And these are "inserted by the compositors without the slightest "compunction". I should say that the great enemy to our understanding these sentences of yours is the want of commas; for though the defective position of words can never be compensated for by commas, they do frequently help to make the sense clearer, and would do so in this instance. How can we certainly know that the words "without the slightest compunction" refer to "inserted"? They seem, by their order in the sentence, to describe the character of the compositors;—they are "compositors without the slightest "compunction". And then that word "*compunc-* "*tion*"; what an ill-chosen word of which to make use when speaking of *punctuation*. But this is in keeping with that which occurs in the first paragraph of your essay, where you speak of persons "mending their *ways*"; and in the very next paragraph you speak of the "Queen's *high-* "*way*", and of "*by-roads*" and "*private roads*".

But to return. Not only do you describe the poor compositors as beings " without any compunc- "tion"; but also as beings "without any mercy". The sentence runs thus: "These 'shrieks', as they "have been called, are scattered up and down the "page by compositors without any mercy". I have often heard of "printers' devils", and I imagined them to be the boys who assist in the press-room; but if your description of compositors is true, these are beings of an order very little superior.

By-the-way, while noticing these ghostly exist- ences, I may just remark that immediately after your speaking of " things without life ", you startle us with that strange sentence of yours—" I "will introduce the body of my essay". *Introduce the body!* We are prepared for much in these days of " sensation " writing; and the very preva- lence of the fashion for that style of composition pre-disposes any one of a quick imagination to believe, for the instant, that your essay on the ' Queen's English ' is about to turn into a '*Strange* ' *Story* '.

"But to be more serious", as you say in your

essay and then immediately give us a sentence in which the grave and the grotesque are most incongruously blended. I read, "A man does not lose "his mother now in the papers". I have read figurative language which spoke of lawyers being lost in their papers, and of students being buried in their books; but I never read of a man losing his mother in the papers; therefore I do not quite see what the adverb "now" has to do in the sentence. Ah! stop a moment. You did not mean to speak of a man losing his mother in the papers. I perceive by the context that what you intended to say was something of this sort:—According to the papers, a man does not now lose his mother;—but that is a very different thing. How those little prepositions "from" and "in" do perplex you; or rather, how greatly your misuse of them perplexes your readers.

With the adverbs also you are equally at fault. You say, "In all abstract cases where we merely "speak of numbers the verb is better singular." Here the placing of the adverb "merely" makes it a limitation of the following word "speak"; and the question might naturally enough be asked, But what if we *write* of numbers? The adverb, being intended to qualify the word "numbers", should have been placed immediately after it. The sentence would then have read, "In all abstract cases "where we speak of numbers merely, the verb is "better singular." So also in the sentence, "I only "bring forward some things", the adverb "only" is similarly misplaced; for, in the following sentence, the words "Plenty more might be said", show that the "only" refers to the "some things", and not to the fact of your bringing them forward. The sentence should therefore have been, "I bring "forward some things only. Plenty more might "be said." Again, you say, "Still, though too "many commas are bad, too few are not without "inconvenience also." Here the adverb "also", in consequence of its position, applies to "incon-"venience"; and the sentence signifies that too few commas are not without inconvenience besides being bad. Doubtless, what you intended was, "Still, though too many commas are bad, too few "also are not without inconvenience."

Blair, in speaking of adverbs, says, "The fact is, "with respect to such adverbs as *only, wholly, at* "*least,* and the rest of that tribe, that, in common "discourse, the tone and emphasis we use in pro-"nouncing them, generally serve to show their "reference, and to make the meaning clear; and "hence we acquire the habit of throwing them in "loosely in the course of a period. *But in writ-* "*ing*", [and I wish you to notice this, because it bears upon a remark in your letter to me,] "*But* "*in writing, where a man speaks to the eye and not* "*to the ear, he ought to be more accurate, and so to* "*connect those adverbs with the words which they* "*qualify as to put his meaning out of doubt upon* "*the first inspection.*"

In my private letter to you, I quoted as the basis of some remarks I had to make, the well-known rule that "those parts of a sentence which are "most closely connected in their meaning, should "be as closely as possible connected in position." In your reply you speak of my remarks as "the "fallacious application of a supposed rule." Whether my application of the rule is fallacious or not, let others judge from this letter; and as to whether the rule itself is only "a supposed rule", or whether it is not, on the contrary, a standard rule emanating from the highest authorities, let the following quotations decide.

I read in Kames's '*Elements of Criticism*', "Words expressing things connected in the thought, "ought to be placed as near together as possible."

I read in Campbell's '*Philosophy of Rhetoric*',

"In English and other modern languages, the "speaker doth not enjoy that boundless latitude "which an orator of Athens or of Rome enjoyed "when haranguing in the language of his country. "With us, who admit very few inflections, the "construction, and consequently *the sense, depends* "*almost entirely on the order.*"

I read in Blair's *'Lectures on Rhetoric and Belles 'Lettres'*, "The relation which the words, or the "members of a period, bear to one another, cannot "be pointed out in English, as in Greek or in Latin, "by means of terminations ; it is ascertained only "by the position in which they stand. Hence a "capital rule in the arrangement of sentences is, "that the words, or the members, most nearly related "should be placed in the sentence, as near to each "other as possible; so as to make their mutual "relation clearly appear."

See also *'Murray's Grammar'*, part 2, in the Appendix; likewise, *'The Elements of English 'Composition'*, by David Irving, LL.D., chapter 7; and the *'Grammar of Rhetoric'*, by Alexander Jamieson, LL.D., chapter 3, book 3.

As an illustrative example of the violation of this rule, take the following sentences. "It con-"tained", says Swift, "a warrant for conducting

" me and my retinue to Traldragdubb or Trildrog-
" drib, for it is pronounced both ways, as nearly as
" I can remember, *by a party of ten horse.*" The
words in italics must be construed with the participle "conducting", but they are placed so far from that word, and so near the word "pronounced", that at first they suggest a meaning perfectly ridiculous.

Again, in the course of a certain examination which took place in the House of Commons in the year 1809, Mr. Dennis Browne said, that the witness had been " ordered to withdraw from the bar in
" consequence of being intoxicated, by the motion
" of an honourable member." This remark, as might have been expected, produced loud and general laughter. The speaker intended to say, that, " in consequence of being intoxicated, the
" witness, by the motion of an honourable member,
" had been ordered to withdraw from the bar."

A similar error occurs in a work by Isaac D'Israeli. He meant to relate that, " The beaux of
" that day, as well as the women, used the abomi-
" nable art of painting their faces "; but he writes, " The beaux of that day used the abominable art
" of painting their faces, as well as the women "!

In your essay, you say, " I remember, when the

"French band of the 'Guides' were in this country, "reading in the *Illustrated News*'". Were the Frenchmen, when in this country, reading in '*The Illustrated News*'? or did you mean that *you* remembered reading in '*The Illustrated News*', when the band of the French Guides, &c?

You say also, "It is not so much of the great "highway itself of the Queen's English that I "would now speak, as of some of the laws of the "road; the by-rules, to compare small things "with great, which hang up framed at the various "stations". What are the great things which hang up framed at the various stations? If you mean that the by-rules hang up framed at the various stations, the sentence would have been better thus, "the laws of the road; or, to compare "small things with great, the by-rules which hang "up framed at the various stations".

So, too, in that sentence which *introduces the body* of your essay, you speak of "the reluctance "which we in modern Europe have to giving any "prominence to the personality of single individ-"uals in social intercourse"; and yet it was evidently not of single individuals in social intercourse that you intended to speak, but of giving, in social intercourse, any prominence to the personality of single individuals. Your language expresses a meaning different from that which was intended: just as does Goldsmith's language when, in the following tautological sentence, he says, "The Greeks, fearing to be surrounded on all "sides, wheeled about and halted, with the river "on their backs." Talk of Baron Munchausen! Why, here was an army of Munchausens. They "*wheeled about and halted, with the river on their* "*backs.*" They might well *halt* under such a load.

An accurate writer will always avoid the possibility of his sentences' having a double meaning; yet the following extract is from a certain journal which started with the avowed intention of setting the rest of the literary world an example of pure English:—"On Saturday morning a man, sup-"posed to be a doctor of philosophy, threw a stick "at the window at which the King of Prussia "was witnessing the *defiling* of a detachment of "soldiers"! This is almost as rich as R. Blair's description of disappointed ambition:—

"Ambition, half convicted of her folly,
Hangs down the *head*, and reddens at the *tale*."
Blair's Grave.

Once more, you say, "When I hear a person "use a queer expression, or pronounce a name in "reading differently from his neighbours, it always "goes down, in my estimate of him, with a *minus* "*sign* before it—stands on the side of deficit, not "of credit." Poor fellow! So he falls in your estimation, merely because when "reading differ-"ently from his neighbours," you hear him "pro-"nounce a name". Would you have him pass over the names without pronouncing them? The fact is, that in the very words in which you censure a small fault of another person, you expose for censure a greater fault of your own. The pronunciation of proper names is a subject upon which philologists are not in every case unanimous; and to differ where the wise are not agreed, if it is a fault, cannot be a great fault; but to publish a sentence like yours, having in it a clause with what the French call a "squinting "construction",[*] is to commit a fault such as no one would expect to find in '*A Plea for the Queen's* '*English*'. The words "in reading", *look two ways at once,* and may be construed either with the words which precede, or with those which follow. We may understand you to say, "pronounce a "name in reading"; or, "in reading differently "from his neighbours". A more striking example

[*] "*Construction louche*".

of this ludicrous error could scarcely have been given.

Dr. Campbell, in speaking of similar instances of bad arrangement, says, "In all the above
" instances there is what may be justly termed
" a constructive ambiguity; that is, the words are
" so disposed in point of order, as to render them
" really ambiguous, if, in that construction which
" the expression first suggests, any meaning were
" exhibited. As this is not the case, the faulty
" order of the words cannot properly be considered
" as rendering the sentence ambiguous, but as
" rendering it obscure. It may indeed be argued
" that, in these and the like examples, the least
" reflection in the reader will quickly remove the
" obscurity. But why is there any obscurity to be
" removed ? Or why does the writer require more
" attention from the reader, or the speaker from
" the hearer, than is absolutely necessary ? It
" ought to be remembered, that whatever applica-
" tion we must give to the words, is, in fact, so
" much deducted from what we owe to the senti-
" ments. Besides, the effort that is exerted in a
" very close attention to the language, always
" weakens the effect which the thoughts were
" intended to produce in the mind. 'By per-

"'spicuity', as Quintillian justly observes, 'care
"'is taken, not that the hearer *may* understand, if
"'he will, but that he *must* understand, whether
"'he will or not.' * Perspicuity, originally and
"properly, implies *transparency*, such as may be
"ascribed to air, glass, water, or any other medium
"through which material objects are viewed.
"From this original and proper sense it has been
"metaphorically applied to language; this being,
"as it were, the medium through which we per-
"ceive the notions and sentiments of a speaker.
"Now, in corporeal things, if the medium through
"which we look at any object is perfectly trans-
"parent, our whole attention is fixed on the object;
"we are scarcely sensible that there is a medium
"which intervenes, and we can hardly be said to
"perceive it. But if there is any flaw in the
"medium, if we see through it but dimly, if the
"object is imperfectly represented, or if we know
"it to be misrepresented, our attention is imme-
"diately taken off the object to the medium. We
"are then anxious to discover the cause, either of
"the dim and confused representation, or of the
"misrepresentation, of things which it exhibits,
"that so the defect in vision may be supplied by

* '*Instit*'. lib. viii. cap 2.

"judgment. The case of language is precisely "similar. A discourse, then, excels in perspicuity "when the subject engrosses the attention of the 'hearer, and the diction is so little minded by "him, that he can scarcely be said to be conscious "it is through this medium he sees into the "speaker's thoughts. On the contrary, the least "obscurity, ambiguity, or confusion in the style, "instantly removes the attention from the senti-"ment to the expression, and the hearer endeav-"ours, by the aid of reflection, to correct the "imperfections of the speaker's language."

In contending for the law of position, as laid down by Lord Kames, Dr. Campbell, and others, I do so on the ground that the observance of this law contributes to that most essential quality in all writings,—perspicuity; and although I would not on any account wish to see all sentences constructed on one uniform plan, I maintain that the law of position must never be violated *when the violation would in any way obscure the meaning.* Let your meaning still be obvious, and you may vary your mode of expression as you please; and your language will be the richer for the variation. Let your meaning be obscure, and no grace of diction, nor any music of a well-turned period, will make amends to your readers for their being liable to misunderstand you.

In noticing my remarks upon this part of the subject, you say, "The fact is, the rules of "emphasis come in, in interruption of your sup- "posed general law of position." Passing over the inelegant stuttering, "*in, in, in*", in this sentence, I reply to your observation. The rules of emphasis, and what you are pleased to call " the *supposed* general law of position", are entirely independent of each other, and can no more clash than two parallel lines can meet. The rules of emphasis do *not* come " *in, in in*terruption of the "general law of position." A sentence ought, under all circumstances, to be constructed accurately, whatever may chance to be the emphasis with which it will be read. A faulty construction may be made *intelligible* by emphasis, but no dependence on emphasis will *justify* a faulty construction. Besides, if the sentence is ambiguous, how will emphasis assist the reader to the author's meaning? Where shall he apply the emphasis? He must comprehend what is ambiguous, in order that what is ambiguous may by him be comprehended, which is an absurdity.

Emphasis may be very useful to me in explaining to you my own meaning, or, in explaining another's meaning which I may understand; but it cannot assist me to explain that which I do not understand. When to correctness of position is added justness of emphasis, your words will be weighty; but when the first of these qualities is wanting, not the thunder of a Boanerges will compensate for the deficiency.

An amusing instance of wrong emphasis in reading the Scriptures was thus given in a recent number of '*The Reader*'. " A clergyman, in the " course of the church service, coming to verses " 24 and 25 of 1 Sam. xxviii, which describe how " Saul, who had been abstaining from food in the " depth of his grief, was at last persuaded to eat, " read them thus : 'And the woman had a fat calf " ' in the house ; and she hasted, and killed it, and " ' took flour, and kneaded it, and did bake " ' unleavened bread thereof: and she brought it " ' before Saul, and before his servants; and they " ' *did* eat ' ".

Continuing my review of your essay, I notice that it is said of a traveller on the Queen's highway, " He bowls along it with ease in a vehicle " which a few centuries ago would have been " broken to pieces in a deep rut, or come to grief "in a bottomless swamp." There being here no words immediately before "come", to indicate in what tense that verb is, I have to turn back to find the tense, and am obliged to read the sentence thus, "*would have been* broken to pieces in a deep "rut, or [*would have been*] come to grief in a "bottomless swamp"; for, a part of a complex tense means nothing without the rest of the tense; therefore, the rest of the tense ought always to be found in the sentence. Nor is it allowable, as in your sentence, to take *part* of the tense of a passive verb to eke out the meaning of an active verb given without any tense whatever.

Further on, I find you speaking of "that fertile "source of mistakes among our clergy, the mispro- "nunciation of Scripture proper names". It is not the "mispronunciation of Scripture proper "names" which is *the source* of mistakes; the mispronunciation of Scripture proper names constitutes the mistakes themselves of which you are speaking; and a thing cannot at the same time be a source, and that which flows from it. It appears that what you intended to speak of was, "that "fertile source of mistakes among our clergy, their "ignorance of Scripture proper names, the mispro- "nunciation of which is quite inexcusable."

Speaking on this subject, I may remark that, as you strongly advocate our following the Greeks in the pronunciation of their proper names, I hope you will be consistent and never again, in reading the Lessons, call those ancient cities Samaria and Pniladelphia otherwise than Samarīa and Philadelphīa.

I was much amused by your attempt to set up the Church '*Prayer Book*' as an authority for the aspiration of the "*h*" in the word "*humble*"; when, on the first page of the '*Morning Prayer*', we are exhorted to confess our sins "with *an* "humble, lowly, penitent, and obedient heart". As for the argument which you base upon the alliterative style of the '*Prayer Book*'; that argument proves too much, to be in your favour; for if, because we find the words "*humble*" and "*hearty*" following each other, we are to believe that it was the intention of the compilers of our beautiful ritual that we should aspirate the "*h*" in "*humble*", as in "*hearty*"; what was the intention of the compilers when, in the supplication for the Queen, they required us to pray that we "may faithfully serve, *honour*, and *humbly* obey "her"?

Toward the end of your essay you say, "*Entail*

"is another poor injured verb. Nothing ever *leads* "*to* anything as a consequence, or brings it about, "but it always *entails* it. This smells strong of "the lawyer's clerk". It was a very proper expression which Horace made use of when, speaking of over-laboured compositions, he said that they smelt of the *lamp;* but it is scarcely a fit expression which you employ, when, speaking of a certain word, you say, this smells strong of the *lawyer's clerk.* Lawyers or their clerks may be *odious* to you, but that does not give you the right to use an expression which implies that they are *odorous*.

Just as we may know by the way in which a man deals with the small trials of life, how far he has attained a mastery over himself; so may we know by the way in which a writer deals with the small parts of speech, how far he has attained a mastery over the language. Let us see therefore how you manage the pronouns.

I begin by noticing a remark which, in your letter to me, has reference to this part of the subject. You say, respecting my criticism on your essay, "Set to work in the same way with our "English version of the Bible, and what work you "would make of it"! To this I reply: Our English version of the Bible is acknowledged to be, on the whole, excellent, whether considered with respect to its faithfulness to the originals, or with respect to its purity and elegance of language. Its doctrines, being divine, are, like their Author, perfect; but the translation, being human, is frequently obscure.* You bid me look at the "he" and "him" in Luke xix, 3, 4, 5. You surely do not defend the construction of these sentences? See what Dr. Campbell says on this subject, in his '*Philosophy of Rhetoric*', book ii, chap. 6. "It is "easy to conceive that, in numberless instances, "the pronoun '*he*' will be ambiguous, when two or "more males happen to be mentioned in the same "clause of a sentence. In such a case we ought "always either to give another turn to the expres- "sion, or to use the noun itself, and not the "pronoun; for when the repetition of a word is "necessary, it is not offensive. The translators of

* "The Dean falls back upon the authority of Scripture in "defence of some of his indefensible positions. But examples of "bad grammar and bad construction can be found in King "James's translation; and all our standard writers, not "excepting even Addison himself, to the study of whose works "we used to be told to give both day and night, have furnished "an abundant harvest of errors for the critics. Yet there is "good writing, and Mr. Moon's is good; and there is bad "writing, and, in spite of the mending, the Dean's is bad."— THE NATION, No. lix, p. 791. [*A New York Journal.*]

"the Bible have often judiciously used this "method; I say judiciously, because, though the "other method is on some occasions preferable, yet, "by attempting the other, they would have run a "much greater risk of destroying that beautiful "simplicity which is an eminent characteristic of "Holy Writ. I shall take an instance from the "speech of Judah to his brother Joseph in Egypt. "'We said to my lord, The lad cannot leave his "'father, for if he should leave his father, his "'father would die.' Gen. xliv, 22. The words "'his father' are, in this short verse, thrice repeated, "and yet are not disagreeable, as they contribute "to perspicuity. Had the last part of the sentence "run thus, 'if he should leave his father he would "'die', it would not have appeared from the ex-"pression, whether it were the child or the parent "that would die".

A little attention to this matter would have saved you from publishing such a paragraph as the following; "Two other words occur to me which "are very commonly mangled by our clergy. One "of *these* is 'covetous' and its substantive 'covet-"'ousness'. I hope some who read *these lines* will "be induced to leave off pronouncing *them* 'covet-"'ious' and 'covetiousness'. I can assure *them* 'that when *they* do thus call *them*, one at least of "*their* hearers has his appreciation of *their* teaching "disturbed".* You have so confusedly used your pronouns in the foregoing paragraph, that it may be construed in ten thousand different ways.

In some sentences your pronominal adjectives have actually no nouns to which they apply. For example, on page 192, "That nation". What nation? You have not spoken of any nation whatever. You have spoken of "the national mind", "the national speech", and "national simplicity", things pertaining to a nation, but have not spoken of a nation itself. So also, on page 195, " a journal "published by these people". By what people? Where is the noun to which this pronominal adjective refers? In your head it may have been, but it certainly is not in your essay.

The relation between nouns and pronouns is a great stumbling-block to most writers. The following sentence occurs in Hallam's '*Literature 'of Europe'* :—" No one as yet had exhibited the "structure of the human kidneys, Vesalius having "only examined them in dogs". *Human kidneys in dogs!* †

* The *italics* are not the Dean's.
† Breen's '*Modern English Literature*'. An admirable work.

In a memoir of John Leyden, the shepherd boy, in '*Small Beginnings; or, the Way to Get On*', there is, on page 104, the following passage:— "The Professor soon perceived, however, that the "intellectual qualities of the youth were superior "to those of his raiment". *Intellectual qualities of raiment!*

In your essay, on page 196, you say, "I have "known cases where it has been thoroughly eradi- "cated". "When I hear a man gets to his *its*", says Wm. Cobbett, "I tremble for him". Now just read backwards with me, and let us see how many singular neuter nouns intervene before we come to the one to which your pronoun "*it*" belongs. "A tipple", "a storm", "the charitable "explanation", "the well-known infirmity", "the "way", "ale", "an apology", "the consternation", "their appearance", "dinner", "the house", "the "following incident", "his *ed*", "a neighbouring "table", "a South-Eastern train", "a Great "Western", "Reading", "a refreshment-room", "the *h*atmosphere", "the hair", "the air", the "cholera", "his opinion", "this vulgarism", "energy", "self-respect", "perception", "intelli- "gence", "*habit*." Here we have it at last. Only twenty-eight nouns intervening between the pronoun "*it*" and the noun "*habit*" to which it refers! I could give additional examples from your essay, but surely this is enough, to show that the schoolmaster is needed by other persons besides the Directors of the Great-Western and of the South-Eastern railways.

One word in conclusion. You make the assertion that the possessive pronoun "*its*" "never " occurs in the English version of the Bible". It is to be regretted that you have spoken so positively on this subject. Probably the knowledge of our translators' faithfulness to the original text, and the fact of there being in Hebrew no neuter, may have led you and others into this error; but look at Leviticus xxv, 5, "That which groweth of " *its* own accord", and you will see that "its", the possessive of "it", *does* occur "in the English " version of the Bible".

I am, Rev. Sir,

Yours most respectfully,

G. WASHINGTON MOON.

THE DEAN'S ENGLISH:

CRITICISM No. II;

IN REPLY TO THE DEAN OF CANTERBURY'S REJOINDER.

WHAT! is it possible that the Dean of Canterbury can have so forgotten the Scriptural precept "*Be* "*courteous*", as to speak, in a public meeting, in such a manner about an absent antagonist, that the language is condemned by the assembly, and the Dean is censured by the public press? Your own county paper, Reverend Sir, '*The South-Eastern* '*Gazette*,' in giving a report of your second lecture[*] in St George's Hall, Canterbury, makes the following observations: "Mr. G. W. Moon issued "a pamphlet controverting many of the points "advanced by the Dean, and showing that the "reverend gentleman himself had been guilty of

[*] Subsequently published in '*Good Words*', June, 1863.

"the very violations of good English which he had
"so strongly condemned in others. The greater
"portion of the Dean's lecture on Monday evening
"was devoted to an examination of the statements
"made by Mr. Moon, and to a defence of the
"language employed by the Dean in his former
"lecture. Opinions differ as to the success of the
"reverend gentleman, many of his positions being
"called in question; while the epithets which he
"did not hesitate to use, in speaking of an antago-
"nist possessing some acquaintance with the
"English language, were generally condemned.
"These might and ought to have been avoided,
"especially by one whose precepts and example
"have their influence, for good or for harm, upon
"the society in which he moves. *Get wisdom, get
"'understanding, and forget it not'*, is a text that
"even the Dean of Canterbury might ponder over
"with advantage".

What, too, is to be said of that language which, even in your calmer moments, you have not scrupled to apply to me? You had, in your former essay,* worded a sentence so strangely, that it suggested a meaning perfectly ludicrous. I called

* '*A Plea for the Queen's English*'.—'*Good Words*', March, 1863.

your attention to this, first in a private letter, and afterwards in a pamphlet,* and, in your '*Plea for 'the Queen's English, No. II*', you indignantly exclaim, in reference to my remarks, "*We do not write "for idiots*". Thank you for your politeness; I can make all excuses for hasty words spoken in unguarded moments; but when a gentleman deliberately uses such expressions *in print*, he shows, by his complacent self-sufficiency, how much need he has to remember that it is possible to be worse than even an idiot. " Seest thou a " man wise in his own conceit? there is more hope " of a fool than of him". Prov. xxvi, 12.

Continuing your remarks on my criticisms, you say, " It must require, to speak in the genteel " language which some of my correspondents " uphold, *a most abnormal elongation of the auri- " cular appendages,* for a reader to have suggested " to his mind a fall from the sublime height of " ignorance down into the depth of a mistake." I spoke of editors falling *into* mistakes: it remained for the Dean of Canterbury to add, that they fell *down* into the *depth* of a mistake. You say you do not write for idiots; who else would imagine that it were possible to fall *up* into a *depth ?*

* The previous letter is a re-publication of that pamphlet.

Reverting to your expression, "*abnormal elonga-*
"*tion of the auricular appendages*",—you recommended us, in your former essay, to use plainness of language, and, when we mean a spade, to say so, and not call it "a well-known oblong instrument "of manual husbandry". I wonder that you did not follow your own teaching, and, in plain language, call me *an ass;* but I suppose that you considered the language plain enough, and certainly it is: there can be no doubt as to your meaning. I must leave it to the public to decide whether I have deserved so distinguished a title. Recipients of honours do not generally trouble themselves about *merit:* but, as I am very jealous for the character of him who has thus flatteringly distinguished me; and as some captious persons may call in question his right to confer the title of *ass;* I shall endeavour, in the following pages, to silence for ever all cavillers, and to prove, to demonstration, that he did not give away that which did not belong to him.

Of my former letter, you say that, when you first looked it through, it reminded you of the old story of the attorney's endorsement of the brief,— "No case: abuse the Plaintiff"; for, the objections brought by me against the matter of your essay, are very few and by no means weighty, as I have spent almost all my labour in criticisms on your style and sentences. Precisely! I wished to show, by your own writings, that, so far were you from being competent to teach others English composition, you had need yourself to study its first principles; but there is no *abuse* whatever in that letter: you had no precedent in *my* remarks for *your* language; and as for my having made but few objections to your essay, I will at once give you convincing proof that it was not because I had no more objections to make.

I had written the following paragraph before your second essay was published; and although, in that essay, you defend the statement which you had previously made, I conceive that you have not by any means established your position.

I venture to assert that, what we say figuratively of some not over-wise persons, we may say literally of you,—"You do not know how the cat jumps"; for, what do you tell us? You tell us that it is wrong to say, "The cat jumped on to the chair", the "to", you remark, "being wholly unneeded " and never used by any careful writer or speaker." With all due deference to so high an authority on so very important a matter, I beg leave to observe that, when we say, "The cat jumped on "to the chair", we mean that the cat jumped from somewhere else *to* the chair, and alighted *on* it; but when we say, "The cat jumped on the chair", we mean that the cat was on the chair already, and that, while there, she jumped. The circumstances are entirely different; and according to the difference in the circumstances, so should there be a difference in the language used to describe them respectively. It is evident that in watching the antics of puss, you received an impulse from her movements, and you yourself *jumped—to a wrong conclusion.*

Again, you say, "I pass on now to *spelling*, on "which I have one or two remarks to make. The "first shall be, on the trick now so universal" ['*so* 'universal'! as if universality admitted of com-

---

* '*The Edinburgh Review*', after objecting to some of my remarks as hypercritical, says, "It is not meant that *all* Mr. "Moon's comments are of this kind. The Dean's style is "neither particularly elegant nor correct, and his adversary "sometimes hits him hard; besides in one or two cases success-"fully disputing his judgments. On the important question "(for instance) whether we should say the cat jumped '*on* "'*to* the chair', or '*on* the chair', we must vote against "the Dean, who unjustly condemns the former expres-"sion."

parison] "across the Atlantic, and becoming in
"some quarters common among us in England, of
"leaving out the '*u*' in the termination '*our*';
"writing *honor, favor, neighbor, Savior, &c.* Now
"the objection to this is not only that it makes
"very ugly words, totally unlike anything in the
"English language before, but that it obliterates
"all trace of the derivation and history of the
"word. The late Archdeacon Hare, in an
"article on English orthography in the '*Philo-*
"'*logical Museum*', some years ago, expressed a
"hope that 'such abominations as *honor* and *favor*
"'would henceforth be confined to the cards of
"'the great vulgar.' There we still see them, and
"in books printed in America; and while we are
"quite contented to leave our fashionable friends
"in such company, I hope we may none of us be
"tempted to join it." I will tell you where else
these "abominations" may be found, besides being
found "on the *cards* of the great vulgar". They
may be found in a volume of poems by Henry
Alford, Dean of Canterbury; a volume published,
not in America, but in this country, by Rivingtons
of Pall Mall. The following is a specimen taken
from his "RECENT POEMS". Two verses will
suffice.

RECENT POEMS.

A WISH.

"Would it were mine, amidst the changes
"Through which our varied lifetime ranges,
"To live on Providence's bounty
"Down in some *favored* western county.

*   *   *   *   *

"There may I dwell with those who love me;
"And when the earth shall close above me,
"My memory leave a lasting *savor*
"Of grace divine, and human *favor*."

It is true that there is a preface to the volume, and that it accounts for the spelling of such words, by informing us that many of the poems have been published in America; but that is no justification of your retaining the Transatlantic spelling which you condemn. I *guess* you do not mean to imply that it is with poems as with persons,—*i.e.*, that a temporary residence abroad occasions them to acquire habits of pronunciation, &c, not easily thrown off on a return to the mother country; and yet, if this is not what the preface means, pray, what does it mean? Perhaps, as certain words are branded on the alpenstocks of mountain travellers, to show the height that has been attained by them, so you have thought well to *favor* us with this *savor* of Americanisms, to show us that your poems have had the *honor* of being republished on the other side of the Atlantic.

It appears to me that the preface serves only to make matters worse; for it shows that the objectionable form of orthography is retained with your knowledge and your sanction, for I have quoted from the "*Third Edition.*" How is this? You say that the spelling in question should be confined to the cards of "*the great vulgar*"; and *you yourself* adopt that very spelling!

Before quitting the subject of the spelling of words of this description, I beg leave to say that although there are, in our language, certain words ending in "*our*", which, as we have seen, are sometimes spelt with "*or*" only; as hon*or*, fav*or*, &c., without interference with the sense, hon*or* being still the same as hon*our*, and fav*or* the same as fav*our*; there is one word of this class, the meaning of which changes with the change of spelling; namely, the word *tenour*, which, with the "*u*", means continuity of state; as in '*Gray's* '*Elegy*',—

" Along the cool sequestered vale of life
" They kept the noiseless *tenour* of their way:"

but without the "*u*", it means a certain clef in music. This distinction has been very properly noticed by Dr. Nugent in his '*English and French 'Dictionary*'; there the words stand thus:—

" Tenor, *alto*, m.
" Tenour, *manière*, f."

but you, after lecturing us upon the impropriety of leaving out the "*u*" in "*honour*", and in "*favour*", although the omission in these words makes no alteration in the sense, yourself leave the "*u*" out of "*tenour*", and speak, on page 429, of the "*tenor*" of your essay! If this is not straining at gnats and swallowing a camel, I do not know what is. What with the *tenor* of your essay, and the *bass*, or baseness, of your English, you certainly are fiddling for us a very pretty tune. It is to be hoped that if we do not dance quite correctly, to your new music, you will take into consideration the extreme difficulty we have to understand the contradictory instructions we have received.

The following remarks upon this subject are from '*The Round Table*', a New York Journal:—
" The mode of spelling this class of words under
" discussion, which is now getting more and more
" established, is only a part of the simplifying

"process which has been going on in the ortho-
"graphy of the English language for two hundred
"and fifty years. Wherever such a process tends
"to obscure the origin of words it ought to be
"checked. But this cannot be said in the present
"case; for *honor* and the like come to us from the
"Latin, and in fact seem to have retained their
"Latin form in French originally, as the following
"lines will show—lines as old as the times of the
"Norman minstrels:

"' Les terres, les ficus, *les honors.*'
"' Des Daneiz firent grant *dolor.*'

"English usage has never been settled or uniform
"with regard to the spelling of words ending in
"*our*. Every one knows this, and yet it will be
"pleasant to illustrate the fact by a few examples.
"Milton, who was always particular about his
"spelling, is wicked enough sometimes to write
"thus:

"'——*honor dishonorable*,
"' Sin-bred, how have ye troubl'd all mankind
"' With shews instead, meer shews of seeming pure,'
"' *Paradise Lost*,' First Edition, Book iv. Line 314.

"I wonder what the old bard would have said if
"Dean Alford had been there to tell him that the
"spelling in the foregoing passage was an 'abomina-

"'tion.' Probably he would have extended to him
"the same polite invitation that Samson did to
"Harapha, namely, just to come within reach of his
"fists. Bacon also does not scruple to spell after the
"same fashion when it pleases him; as is seen
"here: 'In sutes of *favor* the first comming ought
"'to take little place'; 'hee doth not raine wealth,
"'nor shine *honors* and vertues upon men equally';
"where *honors* is the word given in the manuscript.
"It is a little singular that Sidney always addresses
"his letters to the 'Right *Honorable*,' but com-
"monly prefers to say 'your *honour*.'

"Every writer seems to follow his own notions
"about the spelling of words in *our*, and those
"'abominations' in the eyes of Archdeacon Hare
"and Dean Alford have been freely used by the
"best authors through all periods of English
"literature."

You justly censure the editors of newspapers for using the expression "*open up*", and you say, "what "it means more than *open* would mean, I never "could discover". But permit me to say that, if you look at home, you will find in your own periodical, in the identical number of it containing this remark of yours, two Doctors of Divinity using the very expression which you condemn; a third

Doctor of Divinity using an expression very similar; and a fourth, *yourself*, using an expression which, under the circumstances, is deserving of severe censure. To begin with the Editor; the Rev. Norman Macleod, D.D., says, on page 204, "He *opens up* in the parched desert a well that "refreshes us". The Rev. John Caird, D.D., says, on page 237, "Now these considerations may *open* "*up* to us one view of the expediency of Christ's "departure". The Rev. Thomas Guthrie, D.D., says, on page 163, "the past, with its sin and folly, "*rose up* before his eyes". I suppose *you* would say, "What *rose up* means more than *rose* would "mean, I cannot discover". Probably not, but just tell us what *you* mean by saying, on page 197, "Even *so* the language *grew up;* its nerve, and "vigour, and honesty, and toil, mainly *brought* "*down* to us in native Saxon terms". If the word "*up*" is redundant in the quoted sentences of the other learned Doctors, what shall we say of it in *your own?* In their expressions there is sense; so, too, is there in your expression; but it is a kind of sense best described by the word *nonsense.* The language *grew up* by being *brought down!* Sure, it must have been the *Irish* language that your honour was spāking of.

Now for your reply to my letter. In condemnation of your wretched English, I had cited some of the highest authorities ;* and you coolly say, " I must freely acknowledge to Mr. Moon, that not " one of the gentlemen whom he has named has " ever been my guide, in whatever study of the " English language I may have accomplished, or in " what little I may have ventured to write in that " language ". " I have a very strong persuasion " that common sense, ordinary observation, and the " prevailing usage of the English people, are quite " as good guides in the matter of the arrangement " of sentences, as [are] the rules laid down by " rhetoricians and grammarians." Thus we come to the actual truth of the matter. It appears that you really have never made the English language your *study !* All that you know about it is what you have picked up by "ordinary observation"; † and the result is, that you tell us it is correct to say, "*He is wiser than me ;*‡ and that you speak

* Dr. Campbell, Lord Kames, Hugh Blair, Lindley Murray, and others.

† " It is notorious that at our public schools, every boy has " been left to pick up his English where and how he could."— Harrison '*On the English Language*', preface, p. v.

‡ This subject was ably commented on by a writer in the '*English Churchman*'. See Appendix.

of "*a decided weak point*" in a man's character! You must have a decidedly weak point in your own character, to set up yourself as a teacher of the English language, when the only credentials of qualification that you can produce are such sentences as these.

You sneer at "Americanisms", but you would never find an educated American who would venture to say, "*It is me*", for "It is I"; or, "*It is him*", for "It is he"; or, "*different to*", for "different from". And nowhere are the use and the omission of the "h", as an aspirate, so clearly distinguished as in the United States. In confirmation of this statement turn over the pages of that humorous American work, "*Artemus Ward, His Book*", and among all the vulgarisms and misspellings there, you will scarcely ever find that the aspirate "*h*" is omitted.

With regard to the purport of your second essay on the Queen's English, it is, as I expected it would be, chiefly a condemnation of my former letter; but you very carefully avoid those particular errors which I exposed; such as, "Sometimes "the editors of our papers *fall, from their igno-* "*rance*, into absurd mistakes"; and, "A man does "not *lose his mother now in the papers*". There are, however, in your second essay, some very strange specimens of Queen's English. You say, "The one rule, of all others, which he cites". Now as, in defence of your particular views, you appeal largely to common sense, let me ask, in the name of that common sense, How can *one* thing be *an other* thing? How can *one* rule be *of* all *other* rules the one which I cite? If this is Queen's English, you may well say of the authorities which I quoted, "There are more things in the "English language than seem to have been dreamt "of in their philosophy"; for I am sure that they never dreamt of any such absurdities.

In my former letter I drew attention to your misplacing of adverbs; and now you appear to be trying, in some instances, to get over the difficulty by altogether omitting the adverbs, and supplying their places by adjectives; and this is not a new error with you. You had previously said, "If "with your inferiors, speak no *coarser* than usual; "if with your superiors, no *finer*." We may correctly say, "a certain person speaks *coarsely*"; but it is absurdly ungrammatical to say, "he speaks "*coarse*"! In your second essay, you say, "the "words *nearest* connected", instead of "the words "*most nearly* connected"; but this will never do;

the former error, that of position, was bad enough, it was one of syntax; the latter error, that of substituting one part of speech for another, is still worse. I have spoken of your "*decided weak "point*": I will now give another example, a very remarkable one, for it is an example of using an adjective instead of an adverb, in a sentence in which you are speaking of using an adverb instead of an adjective. You say, "The fact seems to be, "that in this case I was using the verb '*read*' in "a colloquial and scarcely legitimate sense, and "that the adverb seems necessary, because the "verb is not a *strict* neuter-substantive." We may properly speak of a word as being not *strictly a* neuter-substantive; but we cannot properly speak of a substantive as being "*strict*". So much for the grammar of the sentence; now for its meaning. Your sentence is an explanation of your use of the word "*oddly*", in the phrase, "would "read rather oddly"; and *oddly enough* you have explained it: "*would read*" is the conditional form of the *verb;* and how can that ever be either *a neuter-substantive,* or a *substantive of any other kind?*

In your former essay you prepared us to expect many strange things; I suppose we are to receive this as one of them. You told us, "Plenty more "might be said about grammar; plenty that would "astonish some teachers of it. I may say some-"thing of this another time." Take all the credit you like; you have well earned it; for you have more than redeemed your promise; you have astonished other persons besides teachers of grammar.

Again, you say, "The whole number is divided "into two classes: the first class, and the last "class. To the former of these belong three: to "the latter, one". That is, "To the former of "these *belong* three; to the latter [*belong*] one"; *one belong!* When, in the latter part of a compound sentence, we change the nominative, we must likewise change the verb, that it may agree with its nominative. The error is repeated in the very next sentence. You say, "There are three "that are ranged under the description 'first': "and one that is ranged under the description "'last'." That is, "*There are* three that are "ranged under the description 'first'; and [*there* "*are*] one that is ranged under the description "'last'." *There are one!* The sentence cannot be correctly analysed in any other way. It is true that we understand what you mean; just as we under-

E 2

stand the meaning of the childish prattle of our little ones; but, because your sentence is not unintelligible, it is not, on that account, the less incorrect.

An esteemed friend of mine, Colonel Shaw of Ayr Castle, in reviewing your first essay on the Queen's English, thus wrote concerning a similar error of yours:—" We find this teacher playing
" with the inaccuracy (so *he* calls it) of saying,
" '*Twice one are two*', and '*Three times three are*
" '*nine.*' In order to prove the grammatical incor-
" rectness of these two assertions, the clever Dean
" alters the form of the expression, and, '*presto!*'
" the juggle is concluded. 'What we want,' says
" the Dean, 'being simply this, that three taken
" 'three times makes up, *is* equal to, nine.' Now,
" admitting this to be correct, Mr. Dean,—admit-
" ting *three* not to be *plural* any more than *one;*
" which is just what you should prove, but is also
" just what you do not *attempt* to prove; never-
" theless, admitting your *improved* premises; yet,
" when we say, in another mode, what you '*want*'
" us to say, if that other mode has a plural
" nominative, the verb must also be plural; and,
" we say, '*three times*' must be plural, and so must
" even '*three*'. For example, I might say of a

"man and his wife,—'they twain *are* one flesh';
"but you, Mr. Dean, might reply to me, as you are
"in fact now doing,—'What we want to say is
"'simply this,—this man *is*, and that woman *is*,
"'one flesh,—makes up, *is* equal to, one flesh'.
"All very good! But as long as we speak of
"them as '*twain*', we must, in order to be gram-
"matical, employ the word '*are*' respecting them."

It appears to me that, before you have finished a sentence, you have forgotten how you began it. You say, "We call a 'cup-board' a 'cubbard', a "'half-penny' a 'haepenny', and so of many "other compound words". Had you begun your sentence thus, *We speak of* a "cup-board" as a "cubbard", of a "half-penny" as a "haepenny", it would have been correct to say, "*and so of* "many other compound words"; because the clause would mean, "and so [*we speak*] of many "other compound words"; but having begun the sentence with, "*We call*", it is sheer nonsense to finish it with, "*and so of*"; for it is saying, "and "so [*we call*] of many other compound words".

Elsewhere you say, "Call a spade 'a spade', not "an oblong instrument of manual husbandry; let "home be 'home', not a residence; a place 'a "'place', not a locality; *and so of* the rest."

What is your meaning in this last clause? The sentence is undoubtedly faulty, whether the words "*and so of*" are considered in connexion with the first clause, or in connexion with the following one. In the former case we must say, "and "[*speak*] so of the rest"; and in the latter case we must say, "and [*let us speak*] so of the rest". In neither case can we use the word "*call*", with which you have begun your sentence.

Here is another specimen of your 'Queen's 'English', or rather, of the *Dean's English;* a specimen in which the verbs, past and present, are in a most delightful state of confusion. You are speaking of your previous essay, and of the reasons you had for writing it; and you say, "If I "had believed the Queen's English to have been "rightly laid down by the dictionaries and the "professors of rhetoric, I need not have troubled "myself to write about it. It was exactly because "I did not believe this, but found both of them in "many cases going astray, that I ventured to put "in my plea."

Now, "*I need not*" is present, not past; and it is of the past that you are speaking; you should therefore have said, "*I needed not*", or, "*I should not* "*have needed*". And the verb "troubled", which you have put in the past, should have been in the present; just as the verb "need", which you have put in the present, should have been in the past; for you were not speaking of what you would not have needed *to have done*, but of what you would not have needed *to do*. The sentence, then, should have been, "If I had believed so-and-so, *I should* "*not have needed to trouble* myself".

I may notice also that, in the foregoing sentence, you speak of rules laid down by the "*dictionaries*" and the "*professors of rhetoric*"; thus substituting, in one case, the works for the men; and, in the other case, speaking of the men themselves. Why not speak either of the "*compilers of dictionaries*", and the "*professors of rhetoric*"; or else of the "*dictionaries*", and the "*treatises on rhetoric*"? Write either figuratively or literally, whichever you please; or write in each style, by turns, if you like; for, variety in a series of sentences, where there is uniformity in each, is a beauty; but variety in a single sentence is merely confusion: witness the following extract from Gilfillan's '*Literary Portraits*':—" Channing's mind was "planted as thick with thoughts, as a backwood "of his own magnificent land." *A backwood planted with thoughts!* What a glorious harvest for the writers of America! says Breen. However, I must not enter upon the subject of *style*, lest I should extend this letter to a wearisome length. Suffice it to say, you do not mean that you found *the professors of rhetoric walking off with the books*; though you do tell us you "*found both* "*of them* [the dictionaries and the professors of rhetoric] *in many cases going astray* ".

Continuing my review, I have to notice that you say, " His difficulty (and I mention it because it " may be that of many others besides him) is that " he has missed the peculiar sense of the preposi- " tion *by* as here used." *Your* difficulty seems to be, that you have missed seeing the *peculiar* sense (*nonsense*) of your own expressions. You tell us that you mention your correspondent's difficulty, because it may be a difficulty of many other persons, besides being a difficulty of *him !*

Finally, as regards my criticisms on your grammar; you say, "The next point which I notice " shall be the use of the auxiliaries '*shall*' and " '*will*'. Now here we are at once struck by a " curious phenomenon." We certainly are ;—the phenomenon of a gentleman setting himself up to lecture on the use of verbs, and publicly proclaiming his unfitness for the task, by confusing the present and the future in the very first sentence which he utters on the subject.

Speaking of the verb "to progress", you say, "The present usage makes the verb neuter", and, "We seem to want it; and if we do, and it does "not violate any known law of formation, by all "means let us have it. True, it is the first of its "own family; we have not yet formed *aggress*, "*regress*, &c., into verbs." If you will allow me to *digress* from the consideration of your grammar to the consideration of your accuracy, I will show that you *transgress* in making this statement. In the folio edition of Bailey's '*Universal Dictionary*', published in 1755, I find the very verbs, "*to* "*aggress*" and "*to regress*", which you, in 1863, say, "*we have not yet formed*". In the same dictionary there is also the verb "*to progress*"; and it is given as a verb *neuter*. So that what you call "*the present usage*" is, clearly, the usage of the *past*; the verb which you say is "*the first of* "*its own family*", is nothing of the sort; "*to* "*aggress*" and "*to regress*", which you say "*we* "*have not yet formed*", are found in a dictionary published in 1755; and the neuter verb which you say "*we seem to want*", we have had in use more than one hundred years! Nor are the verbs *aggress* and *regress* mere "*dictionary words without* "*any authority for their use*". The former is used by Prior in his '*Ode to Queen Anne*'; and the latter is used by Sir Thomas Browne in his '*Vulgar Errors*'.*

I will briefly notice a few of your numerous errors in syntax, &c., and then pass on to weightier matters. You speak of a possibility as being "*pre-* "*cluded in*" the mind. You tell us of "a *more* "*neat* way of *expressing* what would be *Mr. Moon's* "*sentence*". We *express* a *meaning*, or we *write* a "*sentence ;* but we do not *express* a *sentence.* The word seems to be rather a pet of yours; you speak of *expressing a woman !* '*Queer English*' would not have been an inappropriate title to your essays. Then we have "in respect of", for "*with respect to*";† and "*an exception which I cannot well treat*", instead of, "*of* which I cannot well treat "; for it is evident from the context, that you were not

---

* For an account of the origin and gradual development of the words "progress", "digress", "egress," "regress", and "transgress", see an interesting little book, called '*English* '*Roots*', by A. J. Knapp, p. 135.

† This error is treated of at some length in '*Lectures on the* '*English Language*', by George P. Marsh, edited by Dr. William Smith, Classical Examiner at the University of London, pp. 467-9.

speaking of treating *an exception,* but *of treating of an exception.*

The construction of some of your sentences is very objectionable : you say, "I have noticed the "word 'party' used for *an individual, occurring in* "*Shakspeare*", instead of, "I have noticed, in "Shakspeare, the word 'party' used for an indi-"vidual". But how is it that you call a man *an individual?* In your first essay on the Queen's English you said, "It is certainly curious enough "that the same *debasing* of our language should "choose, in order to avoid the good honest Saxon "'*man*', two words, '*individual*' and '*party*', one of "which expresses a man's *unity*, and the other "belongs to man *associated*". It certainly is curious; but what appears to me to be more curious still, is that *you*, after writing that sentence, should yourself call a man "*an individual*".

Again, I read, "The purpose is, to bring the fact "stated into prominence": *stated into prominence!* unquestionably, this should be, "to bring into "prominence the fact stated".

Even when writing on the proper construction of a sentence, you construct your own sentence so *im*properly that it fails to convey your meaning. You say, "The natural order of constructing the "sentence would be to relate what happened first, "and my surprise at it afterwards". Your sentence does not enlighten us on your views of the proper *order* in which the facts should be *related*; it tells us merely that we should relate what first happened, and your subsequent surprise at it. Not one word about the order of relation. We are to relate what "*happened first*", but we are not told what to *relate first*. You should have said, "The natural order of constructing the sentence "would be to *relate first* what happened, and "*afterwards* my surprise at it".

Lastly, on this part of the subject; you say, " Mr. Moon quotes, with disapprobation, my words, " where I join together 'would have been broken "'to pieces in a deep rut, or come to grief in a "'bottomless swamp'. He says this can only be "filled in thus, 'would have been'", &c. I am sure that Mr. Moon never, after mentioning your sentence about "*a deep rut*" and "*a bottomless* "*swamp*", speaks of the sentence being "*filled* "*in*"! That is the Dean of Canterbury's style; he gives a sentence about *eating* and *being full*, and then speaks of the sentence being "*filled up*"! He speaks of people *mending their ways;* and, in the very next paragraph, talks about the *Queen's* "*highway*" and "*by-roads*" and "*private roads*". He speaks of things "*without life*"; and immediately afterwards says that he will *introduce the body* of—his essay.

You will, doubtless, gain great notoriety by your strange essays on the Queen's English; for, in consequence of your inaccuracies in them, it will become usual to describe bad language as "*Dean's "English*". By "bad language", I do not mean rude language; I say nothing about that matter. I mean that, because of your ungrammatical sentences, it will be as common to call false English, "*Dean's English*", as it is to call base white metal, "*German Silver*".

You say, "I have given a fair sample of the "instances of ambiguity which Mr. Moon cites out "of my essay". A *fair* sample! and yet you have made no mention of the instance of the eight-and-twenty nouns intervening between the pronoun "*it*" and the noun "*habit*", to which it refers. A *fair* sample! and yet you have made no mention of the instance of ambiguity in the paragraph about "covetous and covetousness"; a paragraph of fewer than ten lines, yet so ambiguously worded that you may ring as many changes on it as on a peal of bells; only the melody would not

be quite so sweet. However, if you do not object to a little bell-ringing, and if you will not think it sacrilegious of me to pull the ropes, I will just see what kind of a peal of bells it is that you have hung in your belfry, for I call the paragraph, "*the "belfry*", and the pronouns, "*the peal of bells*", and these I name after the gamut, A, B, C, D, E, F, G, so we shall not have any difficulty in counting the changes. You say, " While treating of the pronun-
" ciation of those who minister in public, two
" other words occur to me which are very commonly
" mangled by our clergy. One of *th̊ese* is 'covetous',
" and its substantive 'covetousness'. I hope some
" who read *these lines* will be induced to leave off
" pronouncing *th̊em* 'covetious', and 'covetiousness'.
" I can assure *th̊em*, that when *th̊ey* do thus call
" *th̊em*, one, at least, of *th̊eir* hearers has his appre-
" ciation of *th̊eir* teaching disturbed". I fancy that many a one who reads these lines will have *his* appreciation of *your* teaching disturbed, as far as it relates to the Queen's English. But now for the changes which may be rung on these bells, as I have called them. The first of them, "A", may apply either to "words", or to "our clergy". You say, "*our clergy.* One of *these* is 'covetous'". I

am sorry to say that the general belief is, there are more than *one;* but perhaps you know one in particular. However, my remarks interrupt the bell-ringing, and we want to count the changes, so I will say no more, but will at once demonstrate that we can ring 10,240 changes on your peal of bells! In other words, that your paragraph, of fewer than ten lines, is so ambiguously worded, that without any alteration of its grammar or of its syntax, it may be read in 10,240 different ways! and only one of all that number will be the right way to express your meaning.

	The Pronouns.	Nouns to which they may apply.	No. of Nouns.	No. of Different Readings.	
A	*these*	words, or clergy . . .	2	. . . . . .	2
B	*them*	words, clergy, readers, or lines	4	these 4×by the previous 2=	8
C	*them*	words, clergy, readers, or lines	4	these 4×by the previous 8=	32
D	*they*	words, clergy, readers, or lines	4	these 4×by the previous 32=	128
E	*them*	words, clergy, readers, or lines	4	these 4×by the previous 128=	512
F	*their*	words, clergy, readers, or lines	4	these 4×by the previous 512=	2048
G	*their*	words, clergy, readers, lines, or hearers	5	these 5×by the ,, 2048=	10,240

This is indeed a valuable addition to the curiosities of literature: a treasure " PRESENTED "TO THE BRITISH NATION BY THE VERY REV. THE "DEAN OF CANTERBURY". No doubt it will be carefully preserved in the library of the British Museum.

I have, now, a serious charge to prefer against you; a charge to which I am reluctant to give a name. I will therefore merely state the facts, and leave the public to give to your proceedings in this matter, whatever name may be thought most fitting. You say, on page 439, " I am reminded, " in writing this, of a criticism of Mr. Moon's on " my remarks that we have dropped 'thou' and " 'thee' in our addresses to our fellow-men, and " reserved those words for our addresses in prayer " to Him who is the highest personality. It will " be hardly believed that he professes to set this " right by giving his readers and me the informa- " tion that ' these pronouns are very extensively " 'and profusely [I used no such word] used in " ' poetry, even (!) when inanimate objects are " ' addressed '. and thinks it worth while to quote " Coleridge's Address to Mont Blanc to prove his " point ! Really, might not the very obvious ' notoriety of the fact he adduces have suggested " to him that it was totally irrelevant to the " matter I was treating of?" Truly, this is *the play of Hamlet with the Ghost left out by special desire.* Your object was to controvert what I had advanced against your essay; and, I must say, that the means which you have adopted to accomplish that end, are, to speak mildly, not much to your credit. I will prove what I say. *The one word, against which the whole of my argument was directed, you have, in reproducing your sentence, omitted from the quotation;* and then, of the mangled remains of the sentence, you exclaim, "It will be hardly "believed that he professes to set this right". I professed nothing of the sort; you must know well, that my attack was against *the one word which you have omitted.* That this was the case, may be clearly seen on reference to my former letter,* where that word was, and still is, *printed in italics,* to draw special attention to it. You betray the weakness of your cause when you have recourse to such a suppression.

Nor is the above instance of misquotation the only one in your essay. On page 429, you put into my mouth words which I never uttered; words which express a meaning totally at variance with what I said. You enclose the sentence in inverted commas to mark that it is *a quotation;* and, as if that were not enough, you preface that sentence with this doubly emphatic remark; "*these*

* Page 6.

"*are his words, not mine*". You then make me say that I hope, "as I so strongly advocate our "following the Greeks in the pronunciation of "their proper names, I shall be consistent, and "never again, in reading the Lessons, call those "ancient cities Samaria and Philadelphia otherwise "than *Samarīa* and *Philadelphīa.*" I never had any such thought, nor did I ever express any such wish. These words are *not* mine; nor are they any more like mine, than I am like you. The original sentence, of which the foregoing is a perversion, will be found on page 27 of my previous letter.

But the part of my letter which is most commented upon in your reply, is that which treats of the arrangement of sentences; and, exactly as you suppress, in the instance I have given, the *one important word* on which the whole of the argument turns; so, in the matter of the arrangement of sentences, you suppress the *one important paragraph* which qualifies all the rest! You privately draw the teeth of the lion and then publicly show how valiantly you can put your head into his mouth; thus you not only damage your own character for honesty of representation, but also insult the public whom you address, and who, you imagine, can be deceived by such childish performances. The following are the facts of the case. You say, after mentioning the authorities I had named, "The one rule of all others [!] which " he [Mr. Moon] cites from these authorities, " and which he believes me to have continually " violated, is this: that *those parts of a sentence* " *' which are most closely connected in their meaning,* " *' should be as closely as possible connected in posi-* " *' tion'.* Or, as he afterwards quotes it from Dr. " Blair, *'A capital rule in the arrangement of* " *' sentences is, that the words or members most nearly* " *' related should be placed in the sentence as near to* " *' each other as possible. so as to make their mutual* " *' relation clearly appear' "* You then go on to say, "Now doubtless this rule is, in the main, and " for general guidance, a good and useful one; " indeed, so plain to all, that it surely needed no " inculcating by these venerable writers. But " there are more things in the English language " than seem to have been dreamt of in their philo-" sophy. If this rule were uniformly applied, it " would break down the force and the living interest " of style in any English writer, and reduce his " matter to a.dreary and dull monotony; for it is " in exceptions to its application that almost all "vigour and character of style consist". Would any person—*could* any person—in reading the foregoing extract from your reply to my letter, ever imagine that that letter contains such a paragraph as the following? I quote from page 23, where I say, "In contending for the law of position, as laid "down by Lord Kames, Dr. Campbell, and others, "I do so on the ground that the observance of "this law contributes to that most essential quality "in all writings—perspicuity; and although I "would not, *on any account,* wish to see all sen- "tences constructed on one uniform plan, I maintain "that the law of position must never be violated "*when the violation would in any way obscure the* "*meaning.* Let your meaning still be obvious, and "*you may vary your mode of expression as you* "*please, and your language will be the richer for the* "*variation.* Let your meaning be obscure, and no "grace of diction, nor any music of a well-turned "period, will make amends to your readers for "their being liable to misunderstand you". The existence of this paragraph, by which I carefully qualify the reader's acceptance of Dr. Blair's law of position as a universal rule, you *utterly ignore;* and, with the most strange injustice, you charge me, through sentence after sentence, and column after column, of your tedious essay, with maintaining that all expressions should be worded on one certain uniform plan. Sentences so arranged are, you say, according to "Mr. Moon's rule". Sentences differing from that arrangement are, you say, a violation of "Mr. Moon's rule". With as much reasonableness might you leave out the word "*not*", from the ninth commandment, and assert that it teaches, "Thou *shalt* bear false witness " against thy neighbour."

This being your mode of conducting a controversy, I assure you that, were you not the Dean of Canterbury, I would not answer your remarks. Doubtless, before the publication of this rejoinder, many of the readers of your second essay will have noticed the significant circumstance, that, of the various examples which you give of sentences constructed on what you are pleased to call "Mr. " Moon's rule", but which, as I have shown, is only *a part* of "Mr. Moon's rule", *not one example is drawn from Mr. Moon's own letter.*

You say, "But surely we have had enough of " Mr. Moon and his rules". I do not doubt that you have; but I must still detain you, as the Ancient Mariner detained the wedding-guest, until the tale is told. That being finished, I will let you go; and I trust that, like him, you will learn wisdom from the past:—

"He went like one that hath been stunned,
"And is of sense forlorn:
"*A sadder and a wiser man,*
"*He rose the morrow morn.*"

With respect to the date of the introduction of the possessive pronoun "*its*", which, you said, "never occurs in the English version of the Bible"; and which, as I showed you, occurs in Leviticus, xxv. 5; you shelter yourself under the plea that you meant that the word never occurs in the "authorised edition", known as "King James's "Bible". But, as you did not say either "*author-* "*ised edition*" or "*King James's Bible*", I am justified in saying that you have only yourself to blame for the consequences of having used language so unmistakably equivocal, as you certainly did when you said, "*the English version of the Bible*", and did not mean the English version now in every one's hands, but meant a particular edition published 252 years ago. Speaking of my correction of your error, you say, "What is to be regretted is, "that a gentleman who is setting another right "with such a high hand, should not have taken "the pains to examine the English version as it "really stands, before printing such a sentence as "that which I have quoted". I will show you that my examination of the subject has been sufficiently deep to discover that yours must have been *very superficial*. Speaking of the word "*its*", you say, "Its apparent occurrence in the place quoted is "simply due to the King's printers, who have "modernised the passage". "*Apparent* occur-"rence"! It is a *real* occurrence. Are we not to believe our eyes? As for the "*King's printers*", it was not *they* who introduced the word "*its*" into the English Bible. The first English Bible in which the word is found, is one that was printed at a time when there was *no King on the English throne*, consequently when there were no "*King's "printers*": it was printed during the Commonwealth. Nor was that Bible printed by the "printers to the Parliament". Indeed, it is doubtful whether it was printed in this country. The word "*its*" first occurs in the English version of the Bible, in a spurious edition supposed to have been printed in Amsterdam. It may be distinguished from the genuine edition* of the same

---

* The genuine edition contains most gross errors; for instance, in Rom. vi, 13, it is said, "Neither yield ye your

date, 1653, by that very word "*its*", which is not found in the editions printed by the "printers to "the Parliament", or by the "King's printers", until many years afterwards. So when, in your endeavours to escape the charge of inaccuracy contained in my former letter, you say that the introduction of the word "*its*", into the English version of the Bible, is owing to the "*King's "printers*", you, in trying to escape Scylla, are drawn into the whirlpool of Charybdis!

You speak of my demolishing your character for accuracy. I do not know what character you have for accuracy; but this I know, that whenever I see a man sensitively jealous of any one point in particular of his character, I am not often wrong in taking his jealousy to be a sure sign of conscious weakness in that very point. What are the facts of the case with regard to yourself? I have given several instances of your gross in-accuracy. I take no notice of unimportant mis-

---

"members as instruments of *righteousness*", instead of "*un*righteousness"; and, as if to confirm this teaching, it is said, in 1 Cor. vi, 9, "the *un*righteous *shall* inherit the "kingdom of God"; instead of "shall *not* inherit". Complaint was made to the Parliament; and most of the copies now extant were cleared of the errors by the cancelling of leaves. The spurious edition is comparatively faultless.

quotations of the Scriptures and of my own sentences, though I could mention several of each occurring in your second essay; but what are we to say of the following? It is, if intentional, which I cannot believe, the boldest instance of misquotation of Scripture, to suit a special purpose, that I ever met with. I am sure it *must* have been unintentional; but it is such an error, that to have fallen into it will, I hope, serve so to convince you that you, like other mortals, are liable to err; that the remembrance of it will be a powerful restraint on your indignation, if others should venture, as I have done, to call in question your accuracy. The singular instance of misquotation to which I refer is the following.—Speaking of the adverb "*only*" and of its proper position in a sentence; you say, "The adverb '*only*', in " many sentences, where strictly speaking it ought " to follow its verb, and to limit the objects of the " verb, is in good English placed before the verb. " Let us take some examples of this from the " great storehouse of good English, our authorised " version of the Scriptures. In Numbers xii, 2, " we read, 'Hath the Lord *only spoken* by Moses? " 'hath He not spoken also by us?' According to " some of my correspondents, and to Mr. Moon's "pamphlet (p. 12)*, this ought to be 'Hath the "'Lord spoken *only by Moses?*' I venture to "prefer very much the words as they stand". Now, strange as it may appear after your assertion, it is nevertheless a fact that the words, as you quote them, do *not* occur either in the authorised version, known as King James's Bible of 1611, or in our present version, *or in any other version that I have ever seen;* and the words, in the order in which you say I and your other correspondents would have written them, *do* occur *in every copy of the Scriptures to which I have referred!* So you very much prefer the words as they stand, do you? Ha! ha! ha! *So do I.* When next you write about the adverb "*only*", be sure that you quote *only* the right passage of Scripture to suit your purpose; and on no account be guilty of perverting the sacred text; for these are not the days when the laity will accept without proof, where proof is possible, the statements of even the Dean of Canterbury.

Before closing this letter, I have just one question to ask; it is this: Why do you say that I must have "*a most abnormal elongation of the* "*auricular appendages*"? In other words, Why

* Page 14, in this Edition.

do you call me an ass? I confess to a little curiosity in the matter; therefore pardon me if I press the inquiry. Is it because the authorities I quoted are "venerable Scotchmen", and therefore you conclude that I must be *fond of thistles?*— No? Well, I will guess again. Is it because I *kicked* at your authority?—No? Once more, then, Is it because, like Balaam's ass, I *"forbad the "madness of the prophet"*? *Still*, No? Then I must give it up, and leave to my readers the solving of the riddle; and while perhaps there may be some who will come to the conclusion that the Dean of Canterbury calls me *an ass* because I have been guilty of *braying* at him; there are others, I know, who will laughingly say that the *braying* has been of that kind mentioned in Prov. xxvii, 22.

I am, Rev. Sir,

Your most obedient Servant,

G. WASHINGTON MOON.

NOTE.—The Dean of Canterbury having published a letter exonerating himself from the charge of discourtesy, the following appeared in '*The 'Patriot'* newspaper, in answer to that letter.

THE QUEEN'S ENGLISH.

TO THE EDITOR OF THE PATRIOT.

SIR,—Permit me to say, in reference to the letter from the Dean of Canterbury which you published in the last number of '*The Patriot*', that I heartily join you in your regret that any personalities should have intruded into this discussion on the Queen's English, and I gladly welcome from the Dean any explanation which exonerates him from the charge of discourtesy. But I must say, in justification of my having made those condemning remarks which called forth the Dean's letter, that I was not alone in my interpretation of his language. Those who had the privilege of hearing the Dean deliver his '*Plea*', when there were all the accompanying advantages of emphasis and gesture to assist the hearers to a right understanding of the speaker's meaning, understood the epithets which he employed to be intended for me; and, as such, generally condemned them. My authority is '*The South-Eastern Gazette*', of May 19th, which published a report of the meeting.

The Dean states, in his explanatory letter, that he intended the objectionable epithets not for me, but for the hypothetical reader supposed by me to be capable of the misapprehensions I had adduced. It happens, rather unfortunately for the Dean's explanation, that I had not spoken of any hypothetical reader. *Litera scripta manet,*—judge for yourself. I spoke not of what the Dean's faulty language might suggest to some imaginary reader, but of what it did suggest; and to whom, but to me? The hypothetical reader is entirely a creation of the Dean's. However, as he says that he intended the epithets for this said reader, that is sufficient. I am quite willing to help the Dean to put the saddle on this imaginary "ass"; and I think that the Dean cannot do better than set the imaginary "idiot" on the said ass's back, and then probably the one will gallop away with the other, and we may never hear anything more of either of them.

    I am, Sir,

     Yours most respectfully,

      G. WASHINGTON MOON.

"Instead of always fixing our thoughts upon the points in which our literature and our intellectual life generally are strong, we should, from time to time, fix them upon those in which they are weak, and so learn to perceive clearly what we have to amend."—'*Essays in Criticism*', p. 55.—MATTHEW ARNOLD.

THE DEAN'S ENGLISH.

CRITICISM No. III.

REV. SIR,

It gives me great pleasure to withdraw the charge of discourtesy contained in my former letter to you. I cordially accept the explanation which you have given; and though I cannot quite reconcile your statements with all the facts of the case, I feel sure that the discrepancy is merely apparent, not real; and that you are sincere in saying you did not intend to apply to me those epithets of which I complained. But allow me to remark that for whomsoever they were intended, they are objectionable. Such figures of speech neither add weight to arguments, nor give dignity to language; they serve only to illustrate how easy it is for a teacher of others, to disregard his own lessons, and to become oblivious of the fact that all teaching, like all charity, should begin at home. You say that the obnoxious epithets were intended for some hypothetical person; be pleased to receive my remarks on the said epithets as intended for some hypothetical Dean.

In the collected edition of your essays you have called me your friend. Let me then, as a friend, advise you never again to apply to an opponent, whether real or imaginary, such expressions as "*idiot*" and "*ass*"; lest some of your readers, who read also what you are pleased to call your opponent's "caustic remarks", (*lunar-*caustic, if you like,) should amuse themselves by imagining that they see a parallelism between your case and the case of the old prophet of Bethel, as that was understood by some who heard a clergyman, not remarkable for correctness of emphasis, thus read a portion of the old prophet's history;— " He spake to his sons, saying, 'Saddle me the " 'ass.' And they saddled *him* ". 1 Kings xiii, 27.

Actuated by a sincere love for the language which, it seems to me, you are injuring by precept and by example, I resume my criticisms on your essays. You constitute yourself a teacher of the Queen's English. Were it not so, I should consider any strictures on your language as simply impertinent; but as you have judged it to be right to lecture the public on certain improprieties of expression which have crept into common use; it cannot be out of place for one of the public, whom you address, to step forward on behalf of himself and his companions, to test your fitness for the office which you have assumed; especially if he confine his test to an examination of the language used in the lectures themselves.

The only deviation which I have made from that course is in my second letter. There, noticing your remarks concerning the practice of spelling without the "*u*" such words as "*honour*" and "*favour*", I quote from your '*Poems*' the words so spelt, and add some prefatory remarks of yours concerning them. In your third essay you speak of this circumstance, and you inform me that the words "*honor*" and "*favor*" which I quoted from your '*Poems*', were from that part of the volume which was printed in America, and that it was against such American spelling that you protested in your preface.

Allow me to say, in explanation of my having unconsciously quoted from the American part of the volume, that, as the preface stated that the

G

poems which you had added to the American edition were the products of "*later years*", it was not unnatural for me to believe that they were those headed "RECENT POEMS": and it was from them that my quotations were made. Besides, you call the American part of the volume the "*nucleus*" of the edition: therefore, if I had taken my examples of orthography from the commencement as well as from the end of the volume, I should have been justified in doing so; for, surely, a "*nucleus*" is that *around* which other matter is collected. You do indeed make a strange use of the word when you call 400 pages of a volume of poems the "*nucleus*", and leave only 29 pages at the end, to come under the description of "con- "globated matter"! However, even in those few pages of *English* printing, which, according to your own confession, were under your control, I find the word honour spelt "*honor*", and the word odours spelt "*odors*". The charge, therefore, stands as it did; and your explanation has served only to draw more scrutinizing attention to an inconsistency which otherwise might have passed almost unnoticed.

So you really defend your ungrammatical sentence, "If with your inferiors speak no *coarser* "than usual; if with your superiors, no *finer*"; and you not only defend it, as allowable, but actually maintain that it is "*strictly correct*"; the ground of your assertion being that you have "no "choice" open to you between saying "speak no "*coarser*", and "speak *no more coarsely*"; and you object to the latter expression because you believe it would be ambiguous, owing to the term "*no more*" being capable of meaning "*never again*". Was, then, the sentence, with which I found fault, simply "*Speak no coarser*"? You know that it was not. Why, then, do you, by omitting the latter part of the sentence, try to make it appear that it was? Be assured, that even if you could by such means prove to the careless reader that you were correct, or that, at least, you had some show of reason for your use of the expression which I condemned; you would prove it at a cost of character which would make all good men sigh with regret.

But I will not again charge you with intentional inaccuracy. I prefer to impale you on the other horn of the dilemma by first admitting that your remarks were intended to apply to the whole of the sentence, and then showing the absurdity of your reasoning.

Are you not aware that a weak defence is a

strong admission? It is true that "*no more*" sometimes signifies "*never again*"; but you well know that it never can have that signification when it is followed by "*than*". The phrase "speak "*no more* coarsely" may, indeed, mean "speak "*never again* coarsely"; but "speak *no more* "coarsely *than usual*" could never be understood as "speak *never again* coarsely *than usual*"; for, such a sentence would be without meaning. Besides, if you feared that your sentence would be ambiguous with the expression "*no more than*", why did you use that expression in other parts of your essays? For instance, you say, "The Queen "is *no more* the proprietor of the English language "*than* you or I". A certain word, you say, "ought "*no more* to be spelt 'diocess', *than* cheese ought "to be spelt 'chess'." Where were your scruples about "*no more*" and "*never again*", when you wrote these sentences? As for your having no choice between saying "speak *no coarser* than "usual" and saying "speak *no more coarsely* than "usual"; you certainly had not well considered the subject when you made that remark; for, neither of the expressions is the best that might have been used; indeed, the former is grossly ungrammatical; and, as for the latter, to make it "*right to a t*", you must change the "*no*" into "*not*". The sentence should be written thus, to be correct,—"*If with your inferiors speak not more coarsely than is usual; if with your superiors, not more finely.*"

You tell us that "*than*" governs the accusative case. If that is so, why did you, in the sentence which I just now quoted, write,—"The Queen is "no more the proprietor of the English language "*than* you or *I*"? You are inconsistent. Your precepts and your practice do not agree. According to your own rule you should have said "*than* you "or *me*". If "*than*" governs the accusative, the translators of the Scriptures, too, were wrong in making Solomon say, in Eccles. ii. 25, "Who can "eat more *than I*"? They should have made him say, "Who can eat more *than me?*" but even a child would tell you that such an expression would be absurd, except under the supposition that Solomon was the king of the Cannibal Islands! It is not the circumstance that the pronoun is preceded by "*than*", that determines whether the pronoun is to be in the nominative or in the accusative case. It is the meaning which the writer intends to convey, that determines in which case the pronoun must be. I have given you an example of the proper use of "*than I*"; here is an example of the proper use of "*than me*". Our Saviour says, in Matt. x. 37, "He that "loveth father or mother more *than me* is not "worthy of me". The meaning is obvious; but had our Saviour said "He that loveth father or "mother more *than I*", his words would have suggested the possibility of man's love exceeding Christ's! "*Than*" has nothing whatever to do with determining the case of the pronoun.

In your first '*Plea for the Queen's English*', you laid it down as a rule that neuter verbs should not be qualified by adverbs, but by adjectives; *i.e.* we ought not to say "how nice*ly* she looks", but "how "nice she looks"; because, the verb "*to look*", as here used, is a neuter verb, one not indicating an action, but merely a quality, or a state. Very well; but, unfortunately, your practice mars the good which otherwise might be done by your precept; for, "*to appear*" is as much a neuter verb as is "*to* "*look*" used as above; in fact it is but another form of expression for the same meaning; and yet, after ridiculing "young ladies fresh from school", for saying "how nice*ly* she looks"; you yourself say that the account to be given of a certain inaccuracy "appears still more plain*ly*" from the fact that, &c., &c. If I may be allowed to make a somewhat questionable pun, I will say that it *appears* to me more and more *plain* that you never more notably *missed* your vocation than when you began lecturing "boarding-school *misses*" on the Queen's English.

While remarking on your wrong use of adverbs, I may notice that you say, "our Lord's own use so "frequent*ly* of the term". His use of a particular term may be said to have been *frequent;* but it cannot be said to have been "*frequently*". Transpose the words in your sentence and you will see this at once. "Our Lord's own so frequent*ly* use of "the term"! Surely no boarding-school miss would ever write thus. It is the *verb* that requires the *adverb;* the *noun* requires the *adjective*. He *used* the term *frequently;* but his *use* of it was *frequent*.

In my former letter I advised you, when next you wrote about the adverb "*only*", to quote *only* the right passage of Scripture to suit your purpose. I little imagined that I should catch you with a hook so barbed with sarcasm; but you swallowed the bait, and I have indeed caught you. You have taken my words in their literal signification; and, having withdrawn from your essay the misquoted passage from the book of Numbers, which certainly did *not* suit your purpose, have substituted the fourth verse of Psalm lxii. Is it, then, allowable to select from the Scriptures a particular passage favouring a theory of your own, and not to tell your pupils that the language in the verses immediately before and after that passage is opposed to the lessons you deduce from it? I think not; and I cannot refrain from expressing surprise at your adopting such a course. Besides, how could you hope to succeed when every English layman of the present day follows the example of the noble Bereans of old and searches the Scriptures for himself?

The question between us was concerning the position which the adverb "*only*" should occupy in a sentence. I affirmed that it should be as near as possible to the words which it is intended to qualify; and you, that it may with propriety be placed at a distance from them. In support of your opinion, you brought forward a passage from what you call " that storehouse of good English, the authorized " version of the Scriptures ". I proved that you had grossly misquoted the passage, and that the words were not to be found in the order in which you had written them. With respect to the substituted passage from Psalm lxii, 1 suppose I shall not be communicating information which is quite new to you, if I mention that, in the first six verses of the psalm, the adverb "*only*" occurs four times; and, except in the solitary verse which you quote, it is, in each instance, joined to the words which it is intended to qualify. In the fifth verse we read "Wait thou *only upon God;*" and in the second verse and, again, in the sixth, "*He only* is "my rock and my salvation."

As for the Scriptures' being "a storehouse of "good English", allow me to tell you that there are tares among the wheat. The Bible is no more a storehouse of good English than it is a storehouse of scientific truth. It abounds with errors in grammar and in composition. For an example of these, look at Deut. xvii. 5; but read part of the previous verse :—[If] "it be true, and the thing " certain, that such abomination is wrought in " Israel: Then shalt thou bring forth that man or " that woman, which have committed that wicked " thing, unto thy gates, even that man or that " woman, and shalt stone them with stones, till " they die". In the first place, the conjunction " *or* " being disjunctive, the nominative to the verb " *committed* " is in the singular number; and therefore, as the verb is not in the subjunctive mood, the "*have*" should be "*has*", for a verb should agree with its nominative. Secondly, the phrase "*unto thy gates*" is quite out of place; the meaning intended to be conveyed, is not "*committed that "wicked thing, unto thy gates*"; but, "*thou shalt "bring forth unto thy gates that man or that woman*". Thirdly, "*that woman which*" should be "*that "woman who*". In modern English "*which*" is applied to irrational animals, to things without life, and to infants; and either "*who*" or "*that*" is more appropriate when speaking of persons. We should say either "*the woman who*", or "*the woman that*"; not "*the woman which*". Fourthly, "then shalt thou "bring forth that man *or* that woman, ... and "shalt stone *them*". Had it been "that man *and* "that woman" it would have been quite right to use the plural pronoun; but as the verse stands, "*them*" is certainly improper. Fifthly and lastly, "till *they* die"; clearly the verse is speaking of only *one* person being stoned, either a man or a woman, how, then, can we say "till *they* die"? Here are five errors in four lines. So much for your "*storehouse of good English*". Unquestionably there are, in the Bible, passages which for simplicity, for grandeur, for soul-stirring pathos, for richness of poetic imagery, for climax and for antithesis, are unsurpassed in the language; and, in praise of such passages, I would heartily join you; but, when you wish scholars to accept the Bible as a text-book by which grammatical disputations may be settled, we part company at once.

In a former letter I called attention to your injudicious use of the preposition "*from*"; and I pointed out the necessity for guarding against suggesting any idea which has no real connexion with the matter of which you may be speaking. I gave, as an example of this kind of fault, your sentence, "Sometimes the editors of our papers "fall, from their ignorance, into absurd mistakes". Here the preposition "*from*", immediately following the verb "*fall*", suggests the absurd idea of editors *falling from their ignorance*. In your third essay you repeat the fault, and speak of " archi-" tectural *transition, from* the venerable front of an " ancient cathedral". The sentence runs thus, " A smooth front of stucco may be a comely thing " for those that like it, but very few sensible men " will like it, if they know that in laying it on, we " are proposing to obliterate the roughnesses, and " mixture of styles, and traces of architectural " transition, from the venerable front of an ancient "cathedral." Here, if you perceived that the mere juxtaposition of the words "*transition*" and "*from*" was suggestive of an idea which you by no means intended to convey, you should have separated the words by transposing the last clause of the sentence. It might have been done thus;—"proposing to "obliterate, from the venerable front of an ancient "cathedral, the roughness, and mixture of styles, "and traces of architectural transition." You may say that these are trifles; but, remember, "it is "by attention to trifles that perfection is attained; "and, perfection is no trifle." Besides, to quote your own words, "An error may be, in an ordinary "person, a trifle; but when a *teacher* makes it, it "is no longer a trifle."

In your remarks on "*so*", used in connection with "*as*", you say "'so' cannot be used in the "affirmative proposition, nor 'as' in the negative". If this is correct, why do you yourself use "*as*" in the negative? You say "'its' was never used "in the early periods of our language, nor, indeed, "*as* late down as Elizabeth."

But I suppose it is almost useless for me to address you on the subject of the various niceties of arrangement which require to be attended to in the construction of sentences. You seem to care for none of these things. Yet, believe me, such matters, unimportant as they may appear, contribute in a degree far greater than you imagine, to make up the sum of the difference between a style of composition which is ambiguous and inelegant; and one which is perspicuous and chastely correct.

You evidently entertain some fear lest the study of the rules of composition should cramp the expression of the thoughts! Never was there a more unfounded apprehension; and, in proportion as you are successful in disseminating such notions, do you inflict on our language the most serious injury. Fortunately for that language, the poison of your teaching carries with it its own antidote. They who read your essays on the Queen's English cannot fail to notice the significant fact, that he who is thus strongly advocating the principle that the rules of composition serve no other purpose than to "cramp the expression of his thoughts", does not exhibit that fluency and gracefulness of diction which, if his view of the matter were correct, would necessarily be displayed in his own compositions.

A reviewer in '*The Nonconformist*' writes as follows:—"Away with all needless and artificial " rules, say we, indeed—as energetically as the "most energetic. But the elementary and natural "laws of a language fetter only the impatient or "the unskilful; and in the living freedom with "which genius obeys those laws, is its strength and "mastery shown."

What was Milton's opinion on this subject? Was *he* opposed to rules and maxims? Did *he* think that they served no other purpose than to "cramp the expression of the thoughts"? Quite the contrary.

In the year 1638, Milton, in a Latin letter addressed to an Italian scholar who was then preparing a work on the grammar of his native tongue, wrote as follows: "Whoever in a state "knows how to form wisely the manners of men "and to rule them at home and in war by excellent "institutes, him in the first place, above others, I "should esteem worthy of all honour; *but next to* "*him the man who strives to establish in maxims* "*and rules the method and habit of speaking and* "*writing derived from a good age of the nation, and,* "*as it were, to fortify the same round with a kind of* "*wall, the daring to overleap which, a law, only* "*short of that of Romulus, should be used to prevent.* "Should we choose to compare the two in respect "to utility, it is the former only that can make the

"social existence of the citizens just and holy; but
"it is the latter that makes it splendid and beauti-
"ful, which is the next thing to be desired. The
"one, as I believe, supplies a noble courage and
"intrepid counsels against an enemy invading the
"territory; the other takes to himself the task of
"extirpating and defeating, by means of a learned
"detective police of ears and a light infantry of
"good authors, that barbarism which makes large
"inroads upon the minds of men, and is a des-
"tructive intestine enemy to genius. Nor is it to
"be considered of small importance what language,
"pure or corrupt, a people has, or what is their
"customary degree of propriety in speaking it—a
"matter which oftener than once was the salvation
"of Athens: nay, as it is Plato's opinion that by a
"change in the manner and habit of dress serious
"commotions and mutations are portended in a
"commonwealth, I, for my part, would rather
"believe that the fall of that city and its low
"and obscure condition followed on the general
"vitiation of its usage in the matter of speech; for,
"let the words of a country be in part unhandsome
"and offensive in themselves, in part debased by
"wear and wrongly uttered, and what do they
"declare but, by no slight indication, that the

"inhabitants of that country are an indolent, idly-
"yawning race, with minds already long prepared
"for any amount of servility? On the other hand,
"we have never heard that any empire, any state,
"did not flourish in at least a middling degree as
"long as its own liking and care for its language
"lasted."

So far John Milton—the noble advocate of law and rule, though in virtue of the transcendency of his genius he might have claimed to be above all rules. Now let us have a specimen of your English,—the English of the Dean of Canterbury, who, avowedly, disregards all rules, *fearing they would* "*cramp the expression of his thoughts*"*!*

The following example is taken from your third essay. I read, "'*this*' and '*these*' refer to persons "and things present, or under immediate consider-
"ation; '*that*' and '*those*' to persons and things
"not present nor under immediate consideration;
"*or, if either of these, one degree further removed*
"*than the others of which are used* '*this*' *and* '*these*'".
What can be the meaning of this last clause? The reader can only wonder and guess. Utterly defying all power of analysis, it really makes one uncomfortable to read it; and forcibly recalls the following anecdote told of Douglas Jerrold. "On

"recovering from a severe illness, Browning's
"'*Sordello*' was put into his hands. Line after
" line, page after page, he read, but no consecutive
" idea could he get from the mystic production.
" Mrs. Jerrold was out, and he had no one to whom
" to appeal. The thought struck him that he had
" lost his reason during his illness, and that he was
" so imbecile he did not know it. A perspiration
" burst from his brow, and he sat silent and
" thoughtful. As soon as his wife returned, he
" thrust the mysterious volume into her hands,
" crying out, 'Read this, my dear!' After several
" attempts to make any sense out of the first page
" or so, she gave back the book, saying, 'Bother
"'the gibberish! I don't understand a word of
"'it'. 'Thank Heaven', cried Jerrold, 'then I
"'am not an idiot!'"

Here is another specimen from your essay; I give the entire sentence, which, closing with a period, should be complete in its sense. You say, "The next thing I shall mention, not for its own " sake, but as a specimen of the kind of criticism " which I am often meeting with, and instructive " to those who wish to be critics of other men's " language." It was not until I had long and hopelessly pondered over your sentence, that I

H

discovered what it was you intended to say, and what was the reason of my not instantly catching your meaning. I find that the first clause in your sentence is inverted, and that the punctuation necessary to mark the inversion is incorrect, or rather, is altogether omitted; hence, I read the sentence thus,—" The next thing [which] I shall " mention, not for its own sake, but as a specimen," &c.; whereas your meaning was,—" The next " thing [,] I shall mention, not for its own sake, " but as a specimen," &c.; or, putting the words in their natural order, " I shall mention the next " thing, not for its own sake, but as a specimen," &c. Your hobby of leaving out commas carries you too far; your readers cannot follow you: and if you are going to set aside the rules of punctuation as well as those of grammar, you must give us something better than this to convince us of the advantage to be gained by adopting such a course.

Among other curious matters to be found in your essays, is the somewhat startling information that the expressions "*I ain't certain*", "*I ain't "going*", are not unfrequently used by " educated " persons"! I suppose that you mean educated at college, where the study of English is altogether ignored; but of that, more by-and-by. In the mean time I pass on to the next sentence in your essay. Having told us that the expressions are not unfrequently used by "*educated persons*"; you go on to say, "The main objection to *them* is, that "*they* are proscribed by usage; but exception may " also be taken to *them* on *their own* account". So I should think, if they *will* use such expressions as " I ain't certain ", " I ain't going ".

I see that you still say "*treated*", rather than "*treated of*"; *e.g.* "a matter treated in my former "paper". On a previous occasion I spoke of this error; but I suppose, as you still express yourself in the same way, that you consider the terms synonymous; but they certainly are not. *To treat* is one thing; *to treat of* is another; and it is the latter expression that would convey your meaning. The following sentence will exhibit the difference between the two terms :—"A matter *treated of* in my former " paper was *treated* by you with indifference."

One of the defects noticeable in your essays, is that of making your expressions too elliptical. Brevity is undoubtedly an excellent quality in writing; but brevity should always be subordinate to perspicuity. This has not been attended to in the following sentence, which, singularly enough, happens to be upon the very subject of ellipsis

itself. You say, "Some languages are more ellip-
"tical than others; that is, the habits of thought
"of some nations will bear the omission of certain
"members of a sentence better than the habits of
"thought of other nations" [*will*]. Do you not
perceive that but for the little word "*will*", which
I have added to your sentence, the statement would
be, that "the habits of thought of some nations
"will bear the omission of certain members of a
"sentence better than [they will bear] the habits
"of thought of other nations"?—a truth which no
one will be found to deny; but, at the same time,
a truth which you did not mean to affirm.

What! Not yet over that "*pons asinorum*" of
juvenile writers, the "*construction louche*"? You
were there when I wrote to you my first letter;
and you are there still. This ought not to be;
for, the effect of this error is so ridiculous, and the
error itself may be so easily avoided. You say,
"Though some of the European rulers may be
"females, *when spoken of altogether*, they may be
"correctly classified under the denomination
"'kings'." In this sentence, the clause which I
have put in italics has, what our Gallic neighbours designate, "a squinting construction", it
looks two ways at once; that is, it may be

construed as relating either to the words which precede, or to those which follow. Your former error of this sort was in the *omission* of a comma; this time you have erred by the *insertion* of a comma, and in each case a like result is produced. Had there been no comma after the word "altogether", the ambiguity would have been avoided, because the words in italics would then have formed part of the last clause of the sentence: but as the italicised clause is isolated by commas, the sentence is as perfect a specimen of this error as ever could have been given. Absurd as would be the sentence, its construction is such, that we may understand you to say, "Some of the European "rulers may be females, when spoken of alto-"gether"; or we may understand you to say, "when spoken of altogether, they may be correctly "classified under the denomination 'kings'"; but, even in this last clause, it is evident that you say one thing and mean another. The context shows that what you meant, was, "they may *correctly be* "classified", not "they may *be correctly* classified". Slight as is the apparent difference here, the real difference is very great. If I say, "they may *be* "*correctly* classified", my words mean that the classification may be made in a correct manner;

but if I say, "they may *correctly be* classified", the meaning is, that it is correct to classify them. In the first example, the adverb qualifies the past participle "classified"; in the second, it qualifies the passive verb to "be classified"; or, in other words, the adverb in the former instance describes the thing as being properly done; and, in the latter instance, as being a thing proper to do.

One word more before we finish with this strange sentence of yours. On page 59 I had to ask you why, when speaking of a man, you used the slang expression, "*an individual*". I have here, to ask you a question which is still graver. Why, when speaking of women, and one of those the highest lady in the land, do you apply to them the most debasing of all slang expressions? You speak of "*some of the European rulers*", (there are but two to whom your words *can* refer;—our own Sovereign Lady, and the Queen of Spain,) and you describe them by an epithet which cannot appropriately be used except concerning the sex of animals!—they are, you tell us,—"*females*"! I am sure that all who desire your welfare will join me in hoping that Her Majesty will not see your book. It is but too evident that in condemning these slang phrases, as you do in your '*Queen's*

'*English*', page 246, you are echoing the sentiments of *some other writer*, rather than expressing your own abhorrence of slang. I shall be glad if you are able to inform me that I am in error respecting this; and that you have not been *quoting*, but have been giving us original matter.

Reverting to the error occasioned by a comma in the former part of your sentence, I may give, as an other example of the importance of correct punctuation, an extract from a letter in '*The 'Times*' of June 19th, 1863. There, simply by the placing of the smallest point, a comma, before, instead of after, one of the smallest words in the language, the word " on ", the whole meaning of the sentence is altered, and it is made to express something so horrible that the reader shudders at the mere suggestion of it.

The letter is on the American war, and the writer says, "The loss of life will hardly fall short " of a quarter of a million; and how many more " were better with the dead than doomed to crawl, " on the mutilated victims of this great national " crime!" He meant to say,—" than doomed to " crawl on, the mutilated victims of this great " national crime."

While pointing out this solitary error, I emphatically protest against the injustice of your remarks concerning the general inaccuracy of the composition of 'The Times.' I hold that, to those persons who are desirous of perfecting themselves in the English language, there can be recommended no better course of study than the constant perusal of the leading articles in our principal daily paper. That faults are to be found even there, occasionally, must be admitted; but they are very few. The style, varying according to the subject under consideration, is familiar without being coarse, and dignified without being ostentatious. The language is powerful, yet is never marred by invectives; trenchant, yet never at the sacrifice of courtesy. Free alike from vulgarism and slovenliness on the one hand, and from formality and pedantry on the other, it may safely be taken by the student, as a model on which to form a style that will enable him to express his thoughts with grace, precision, and persuasiveness.

But I must hasten to the conclusion of my letter. You say, "The derivation of the word, as "well as the usage of the great majority of "English writers, *fix* the spelling the other way": *i.e. This* (as well as that) *fix it!* Excuse me, but I must ask why you write thus, even though by putting the question, I put you "*in a fix*" to answer it.

You speak of "the *final* 'u' in tenour", and "the *final* 's' in months". You might just as reasonably speak of the *final* "A" in the alphabet.

These errors are so gross that I cannot forbear reproving you in your own words. "*Surely it is an evil for a people to be daily accustomed to read English expressed thus obscurely and ungrammatically: it tends to confuse thought, and to deprive language of its proper force, and by this means to degrade us as a nation in the rank of thinkers and speakers.*"

In your second essay you are loud in praise of variety in composition; and variety enough you undoubtedly have given us; but, unfortunately, the *variety* is not of that description which, in our school days, writing-masters made us describe in our copy-books as "*charming*". We have found, in your Essays on the Queen's English, errors in the use of pronouns; errors in the use of nouns, both substantive and adjective; errors in the use of verbs and of adverbs; and errors in the use of prepositions. There are errors in composition, and errors in punctuation; errors of ellipsis, and errors of redundancy; specimens of ambiguity, and specimens of squinting constructions; specimens of slang, and specimens of misquotation of an opponent's words; and, worst of all, a specimen of a misquotation of Scripture. Add to this the following specimens of tautology and tautophony, and the list will, I think, be complete.

As you have introduced into your essays the short preface to your Poems, that preface becomes fairly amenable to criticism, and I remark that in it you say, "This will *account for* a few specimens "of Transatlantic orthography *for* which the "author must not be *accounted* responsible".

The following is from your third essay:—"An "officer whose duty it is to keep a *counter*-roll, or "check on the *accounts* of others. It seems also "clear, from this *account* of the word, that it "ought not," &c.

Then I read, "One word *on* ' this ' and ' that ', "as we pass *onward*".

"At last we *abated* the nuisance by enacting, "that in future the *debatable* first syllable should "be dropped".

"Thought and speech have ever been freer in "England than in *other* countries. From these "and *other* circumstances, the English language "has become more idiomatic than most *others*".

"The sentences which I have quoted are but a "few *out* of the countless *in*stances *in* our best "writers, and *in* their most chaste and beautiful "passages, *in* which this usage occurs. On ex- "amining *into* it, we find"—&c., &c.

Enough! It was my intention to say a few words of caution to students of the Queen's English, on your advice to them to disregard the rules of grammarians and be guided by custom and common sense; but, on second thoughts, I am sure that any further remarks must be unnecessary; for if your plan cannot do more for its teacher, there need be no fear that it will be followed by any sagacious pupil.

I had fully intended to speak also on the necessity of a more thorough study of English at our Universities; but any remarks on that, will likewise be considered needless; for, your own English is, itself, a volume on the subject.

Nevertheless, read what appeared in the '*Cornhill* '*Magazine*' for May, 1861:—"In Greek and Latin, "no doubt, the clergy have advanced as fast as their "age, or faster. University men now write Greek "Iambics, as every one knows, rather better than "Sophocles, and would no more think of violating "the Pause than of violating an oath. A good

"proportion of them are also perfectly at home in
"the calculation of perihelions, nodes, mean
"motions, and other interesting things of the same
"kind, which it is unnecessary to specify more
"particularly. So far the clergy are at least on a
"level with their age. But this is all that can be
"said. *When we come to their mother-tongue a
"different story is to be told.* Their English—the
"English of their sermons—is nearly where it was
"a hundred years ago. The author of '*Twenty
"'years in the Church*' makes the driver of a coach
"remark to his hero, that *young gentlemen from
"college preparing to take orders appear to have
"learned everything except their own language.*
"And so they have. Exceptions, of course, there
"are, many and bright; but in the main the charge
"is true. The things in which, compared with
"former ages, they excel so conspicuously, *are the
"very things which have least concern with their
"special calling.* The course of their progress has
"reversed the course of charity;—it began abroad,
"and has never yet reached home."

There are, however, a few English scholars who are patriotically fighting under the banner of their own country against the supremacy of foreign languages in our schools and our colleges; and fore-

most among that few is the English lecturer at Corpus Christi College, Cambridge,—the Rev. Alex. J. D. D'Orsey, B.D.; a man of great ability, and one who, for his persevering efforts to awaken an interest in the study of the English language and obtain for it in our Universities that place of honour to which it is entitled, deserves the highest praise. He draws a melancholy picture, but a true one, when, in his *Plea for the study of the English Language*', he writes ;—" To such as can hardly believe, that in
" our Public Schools, Colleges, and Universities,
" there is not the slightest special training in
" English, even for those who are about to enter
" Holy Orders, I can only say that, however sur-
" prising it may seem, it is the simple fact. Some
" have said, that no English teaching is needed in
" our Universities, for men are sufficiently in-
" structed in the language when they 'come up'.
" I meet this by a simple denial, adding that most
" men are not sufficiently instructed *even when they*
" '*go down*'. I appeal to College Tutors, Examiners,
" Bishops' Chaplains, and to the Public, whether
" I exaggerate or not in making this assertion."

Read also the '*Report of Her Majesty's Commis-
'sioners appointed to inquire into the management
'of certain Colleges and Schools*'. (Presented to Parliament by command of Her Majesty, March,

1864.) The following is from the Report of the examination of the head master of Eton, "the greatest "and most influential of our Public Schools."

"*Question*, No. 3530. [Lord Clarendon.] 'What "'measures do you now take to keep up English at "'Eton?'—'There are none at present, except "'through the ancient languages.'

"*Question*, No. 3531. 'You can scarcely learn "'English reading and writing through Thucy- "'dides?'—'No.'

"*Question*, No. 3532. [Sir S. Northcote.] 'You "'do not think it is satisfactory?'—'No; the "'English teaching is not satisfactory, and as a "'question of precedence, I would have English "'taught before French.'

"*Question*, No. 3533. '*You do not consider that* "'*English is taught at present?*'—'*No.*'"

What a disgrace to us as Englishmen is this!—that our noble language,—the language of our prayers to the Throne of Heaven; the language of the dearest and holiest relationships of life; the language of the maternal lips which have blessed us and are now silent in the grave; the language of our sorrows and our joys, our aspirations and our regrets; the language in which we breathe our consolations to the dying and our farewells to those whom we love; the language in which are embalmed the stirring appeals of our patriots and the thrilling battle-cries of our warriors; the language of our funeral dirges over those who have fallen in defence of our homes, our children, and our liberties; the language in which have been sung our pæans of triumph in the hours of victories which have made England great among the nations; that this language,—the language of Shakspeare, of Milton, and of the Bible, should be utterly ignored as a study in our schools and our colleges! This is indeed a disgrace; a disgrace such as was never incurred by the Greeks and Romans; and one upon which men in future ages of the world will look back with wonder.

Ah! Doctor Alford, we find you guilty of injuring by your example and your influence a glorious inheritance, such as has been bequeathed to no other nation under heaven.*

I can believe that the English language is destined to be that in which shall arise, as in one universal temple, the utterance of the worship of

---

* Grimm says, "The English tongue possesses a veritable "power of expression, such as, perhaps, never stood at the "command of any other language of man."—'*Ursprung der* '*Sprache,* p. 52.

"Take it all in all, it is the grandest and the richest of "modern tongues."—'*Edinburgh Review,*' July, 1864, p. 176.

all hearts. Broad and deep have the foundations been laid; and so vast is the area which they cover, that it is co-extensive with the great globe itself. For centuries past, proud intellectual giants have laboured at this mighty fabric; and still it rises, and will rise for generations to come: and on its massive stones will be inscribed the names of the profoundest thinkers, and on its springing arches the records of the most daring flights of the master minds of genius, whose fame was made enduring by their love of the Beautiful and their adoration of the All Good. In this temple the Anglo-Saxon mosaic of the sacred words of truth will be the solid and enduring pavement; the dreams of poets will fill the rich tracery of its windows with the many-coloured gems of thought; and the works of lofty philosophic minds will be the stately columns supporting its fretted roof, whence shall hang, sculptured, the rich fruits of the tree of knowledge, precious as "apples of "gold",—"the words of the wise".

I am, Rev. Sir,

Yours most respectfully,

G. WASHINGTON MOON.

Note.—Since the publication of the previous edition of these letters, I have discovered, in a back number of '*The Edinburgh Review*', the following passage on the prospects of the English language :—

"The time seems fast approaching when the English "language will exercise over the other languages of the "world a predominance which our forefathers little dreamt "of. The prospects of the English language are now the "most splendid that the world has ever seen. The entire "number of persons who speak certain of the languages "of Northern Europe,—languages of considerable literary "repute,—is not equal to the number simply added every "year, by the increase of population, to those who speak "the English language in England and America alone. "There are persons now living[*] who will in all probability "see it the vernacular language of one hundred and fifty "millions of the earth's civilized population.

"Although French is spoken by a considerable propor-"tion of the population in Canada, and although in the "United States there is a large and tolerably compact body "of German-speaking Germans, these languages must "gradually melt away, as the Welsh and the Gaelic have "melted away before the English in our own island. The "time will speedily be here when a gigantic community in "America,—besides rising and important colonies in "Africa and Australia,—will speak the same language, "and that the language of a nation holding a high position "among the empires of Europe. When this time shall

[*] 1859.

"have arrived, the other languages of Europe will be
"reduced to the same relative position with regard to the
"predominant language, as that in which the Basque
"stands to the Spanish, or the Finnish to the Russian.

"For such predominance the English language pos-
"sesses admirable qualifications; standing, as it does,
"midway between the Germanic and the Scandinavian
"branches of the ancient Teutonic, and also uniting the
"Teutonic with the Romanic in a manner to which no
"other language has any pretension. A prize was given
"in 1796 by the Academy at Berlin for an essay on the
"comparison of fourteen ancient and modern languages of
"Europe, and in that essay the author, Jenisch, assigns
"the palm of general excellence to the English; it has
"also been allowed by other German critics that in regard
"to the qualifications which it possesses for becoming a
"general interpreter of the literature of Europe, not even
"their own language can compete with it."—'*Edinburgh
Review*', vol. cix, p. 375,6.

THE DEAN'S ENGLISH.

CRITICISM No. IV.

EXAMPLE *versus* PRECEPT.

Rev. Sir,

A very few more words, and then I close this controversy. You said in '*Good Words*' for 1863, page 437, "*The less you turn your words "right or left to observe Mr. Moon's rules, the better*". It will provoke a smile on the face of the reader to be told that although, you give this advice to *others*, you have, in your second edition, altered and struck out, altogether, not fewer than eight-and-twenty passages which, in their original form, I condemned as faulty.

It is scarcely requisite to say that "*altered*" does not necessarily imply "*corrected*". For example, in 'Good Words' you wrote,—"You perhaps have "heard of the barber who, while operating on a "gentleman, expressed his opinion, that, after all, "the cholera was in the *hair*." As "altered", the sentence runs thus,—"We remember in Punch the "barber who, while operating", &c. This, of course, suggests the idea that Punch, besides being a wit, and a satirist, is also a barber, and that he operates not only upon human consciences but also upon human chins!

You will very likely put in your irresistible plea, —"We do not write for idiots"; but, seeing that you are always trying to make us believe that the style which you advocate is one pre-eminent for its direct and simple clearness, why did you not say, —"We remember reading in '*Punch*,' of the barber who," &c.? This would have been much more perspicuous.

For the entertainment of the curious in such matters, the original passages, published in '*Good Words*' and condemned in the '*Dean's English*', and the altered passages, as they now appear in the second edition of your '*Queen's English*', are subjoined in parallel columns.

THE DEAN'S ENGLISH.

I.

"So far from its being 'so well 'known a fact' that we reserve the singular pronouns 'thou' and 'thee' '*entirely* for our addresses in prayer 'to Him who is the highest Person-'ality', it is not a fact."—p. 6.

THE QUEEN'S ENGLISH.

Struck out

II.

"You say, 'The great enemies 'to understanding anything printed 'in our language are the commas. 'And these are inserted by the 'compositors without the slightest 'compunction.' I should say that the great enemy to our understanding these sentences of yours is the want of commas."—p. 11.

A comma has been inserted between " compositors " and "without the slight-" est compunction ".—p. 99.

III.

"You speak of persons 'mending 'their *ways*'; and in the very next paragraph you speak of 'the Queen's '*highway*', and of '*by-roads*' and '*private roads*'".—p. 11.

Struck out.

IV.

"Immediately after your speaking of 'things without life', you

THE DEAN'S ENGLISH.	THE QUEEN'S ENGLISH.
startle us with that strange sentence of yours,—'I will introduce 'the body of my essay'. *Introduce the body!*"—p. 12.	Struck out.

V.

"'But to be more serious', as you say in your essay, and then immediately give us a sentence in which the grave and the grotesque are most incongruously blended. I read, '*A man does not lose his mother now in the papers.*' I have read figurative language which spoke of lawyers being lost in their papers, and of students being buried in their books; but I never read of a man losing his mother in the papers."—p. 12.

"In the papers, a man does not now lose his mother."—p. 251.

VI.

"In the sentence, '*I only bring 'forward some things*', the adverb 'only' is similarly misplaced; for, in the following sentence, the words 'Plenty more might be said', show that the 'only' refers to the 'some 'things', and not to the fact of your

THE DEAN'S ENGLISH.	THE QUEEN'S ENGLISH.
bringing them forward. The sentence should therefore have been, 'I bring forward some things only'". —p. 14.	Struck out.

VII.

"In your essay, you say, '*I remember, when the French band of 'the 'Guides' were in this country, 'reading in the 'Illustrated News''*'. Were the Frenchmen, when in this country, reading in '*The Illustrated ''News*'? or did you mean that *you* remembered reading in '*The Illustrated News*'"?—p. 17.	"I remember, when the French band of the 'Guides' were in this country, *to have* read in the 'Illustrated News'".—p. 249.

VIII.

"You also say, '*It is not so much 'of the great highway itself of the 'Queen's English that I would now 'speak, as of some of the laws of the 'road; the by-rules, to compare small 'things with great, which hang up 'framed at the various stations*'. What are the great things which hang up framed at the various stations?"—p. 18	"The bye-rules, so to speak, which hang up framed at the various stations."—p. 5.

THE DEAN'S ENGLISH.

IX.

"So, too, in that sentence which *introduces the body* of your essay, you speak of '*the reluctance which 'we in modern Europe have to giving 'any prominence to the personality 'of single individuals in social inter-'course*'; and yet it was evidently not of single individuals in social intercourse that you intended to speak, but of giving, in social intercourse, any prominence to the personality of single individuals."—p. 18.

X.

"Continuing my review of your essay, I notice that it is said of a traveller on the Queen's highway, '*He bowls along it with ease in a 'vehicle, which a few centuries ago 'would have been broken to pieces in 'a deep rut, or come to grief in a 'bottomless swamp*'. There being here no words immediately before '*come*', to indicate in what tense that verb is, I have to turn back to find the tense, and am obliged to read the sentence thus, '*would have

THE QUEEN'S ENGLISH.

Struck out.

"He bowls along it with ease in a vehicle, which a few centuries ago would have been broken to pieces in a deep rut, or *would have* come to grief in a bottomless swamp."—p. 2.

THE DEAN'S ENGLISH.	THE QUEEN'S ENGLISH.
'*been* broken to pieces in a deep 'rut, or [would have been] come to 'grief in a bottomless swamp'".—p. 25.	
XI. "Further on, I find you speaking of '*that fertile source of mistakes among our clergy, the mispronunciation of Scripture proper names*'. It is not the mispronunciation of 'Scripture proper names' which is the *source* of mistakes; the mispronunciation of Scripture proper names constitutes the mistakes themselves of which you are speaking; and a thing cannot at the same time be a source, and that which flows from it."—p. 26.	Struck out.
XII. "In some sentences your pronominal adjectives have actually no nouns to which they apply. For example, you say, '*a journal published by these people*'. By what people? Where is the noun to which this pronominal adjective refers? In your head it may have been, but it certainly is not in your essay."—p. 31.	"A journal published by *the advocates of this change.*"

THE DEAN'S ENGLISH.	THE QUEEN'S ENGLISH.
XIII.	
"Only eight-and-twenty nouns intervening between the pronoun '*it*' and the noun '*habit*' to which it refers!"—p. 32.	The paragraph has been entirely reconstructed.—p. 42.
XIV.	
"You make the assertion that the possessive pronoun '*its*' 'never occurs in the '*English version of 'the Bible*'. Look 'at Leviticus xxv, 5, 'That which groweth of *its* 'own accord'".—p. 33.	"In the English version of the Bible, *made in its present authorized form in the reign of James I.*"—p. 7.
XV.	
"There are, in your second essay, some very strange specimens of Queen's English. You say, '*The 'one rule, of all others, which he 'cites*'. Now as, in defence of your particular views, you appeal largely to common sense, let me ask, in the name of that common sense, how can *one* thing be *another* thing? How can *one* rule be *of* all *other* rules the one which I cite?"—p. 48.	"The one rule which is supposed by the ordinary rhetoricians to regulate the arrangement of words in sentences, is," &c.—p. 123.

THE DEAN'S ENGLISH.

XVI.

"You say, '*The verb is not a 'strict neuter-substantive*'. Your sentence is an explanation of your use of the word '*oddly*', in the phrase, 'would read rather oddly'; and *oddly enough* you have explained it: '*would read*' is the conditional form of the *verb*; and how can that ever be either a *neuter-substantive*, or a *substantive* of any other kind?"—p. 50.

XVII.

"Again, you say, '*The whole 'number is divided into two classes: 'the first class, and the last class. To 'the former of these belong three: to 'the latter, one*'. That is, 'To the 'former of these *belong* three; to 'the latter [*belong*] one'; *one belong!* When, in the latter part of a compound sentence, we change the nominative, we must likewise change the verb, that it may agree with its nominative."—p. 51.

XVIII.

"The error is repeated in the very next sentence. You say, '*There are three that are ranged*

THE QUEEN'S ENGLISH.

In a previous paragraph we now read of a verb, "*of that class called* neuter-substantive, *i.e.*, neuter, and akin in construction to the verb-substantive *to be*."—p. 206.

"To the former of these belong three: to the latter *belongs* one."—p. 146.

THE DEAN'S ENGLISH.

THE QUEEN'S ENGLISH.

'*under the description 'first': and one that is ranged under the description 'last'*'*.* That is, '*There are three that are ranged under the description 'first'; and [there are] one that is ranged under the description 'last.'' There are one!*''—p. 51.

"There are three that are ranged under the description 'first'; and *there is* one that is ranged under the description 'last'".—p. 146.

XIX.

"It appears to me that, before you have finished a sentence, you have forgotten how you began it. Here is another instance. You say, '*We call a 'cup-board' a 'cubbard', a 'half-penny' a 'haepenny', and so of many other compound words*'. Had you begun your sentence thus, '*We speak* of a 'cup-board' as a '*cubbard*', of a 'half-penny' as a '*haepenny*', it would have been correct to say, '*and so of* many other compound words'; because the clause would mean, 'and so [*we speak*] of many other compound words'; but having begun the sentence with '*We call,*' it is sheer nonsense to finish it with '*and so of*'; for it is saying, 'and so [*we call*] of many other compound words'".—p. 53

"We call a 'cup-board' a 'cubbard', a 'half-penny' a 'hae-'pny', and *we similarly contract* many other compound words."—p. 53.

THE DEAN'S ENGLISH.	THE QUEEN'S ENGLISH.

XX.

"You speak of rules laid down 'by the *dictionaries*' and by the '*pro-* '*fessors of rhetoric*'; thus substituting, in one case, the works for the men; and, in the other case, speaking of the men themselves. Why not speak either of the '*com-* '*pilers of dictionaries*' and the '*pro-* '*fessors of rhetoric*'; or else of the '*dictionaries*' and the '*treatises on* '*rhetoric*'?"—p. 55.

Struck out.

XXI.

"The construction of some of your sentences is very objectionable: you say, '*I have noticed the word* '"*party*' *used for an individual,* '*occurring in Shakspeare*'; instead 'of, 'I have noticed, in Shakspeare, 'the word 'party' used for an 'individual.' But how is it that you call a man '*an individual*'?"—p. 59.

"The word 'party', for *a man*, occurs in Shakspeare."—p. 246.

XXII.

" You say, 'While treating of 'the pronunciation of those who 'minister in public, two other

THE DEAN'S ENGLISH.	THE QUEEN'S ENGLISH.
'words occur to me which are very 'commonly mangled by our clergy. 'One of *these* is 'covetous', and its 'substantive 'covetousness'. I hope 'some who read *these lines* will be 'induced to leave off pronouncing '*them* 'covetious', and 'covetious-''ness'. I can assure *them*, that 'when *they* do thus call *them*, one, 'at least, of *their* hearers has his 'appreciation of *their* teaching dis-'turbed'. I fancy that many a one who reads these lines will have *his* appreciation of *your* teaching disturbed."—p. 62.	" I hope *that* some *of my clerical readers* will be induced to leave off pronouncing them 'covetious' and ' covetiousness '. I can assure them, that when they do thus call *the words*," &c. —p. 63.

XXIII.

" Speaking of the word '*its*', you say, '*Its apparent occurrence in the* '*place quoted is simply due to the* '*King's printers, who have modern-*'*ised the passage*'. '*Apparent* occur-'rence'! It is a *real* occurrence. Are we not to believe our eyes?"—p. 71.

Struck out.

XXIV.

" As for the '*King's printers*', it was not they who introduced the word '*its*' into the English Bible.

THE DEAN'S ENGLISH.	THE QUEEN'S ENGLISH.
The first English Bible in which the word is found, is one that was printed at a time when there was *no King on the English throne,* consequently when there were no 'King's printers': it was printed during the Commonwealth."—p. 71.	"An alteration by *the printers.*"—p. 7.

XXV.

"The following is, if intentional, which I cannot believe, the boldest instance of misquotation of Scripture, to suit a special purpose, that I ever met with. You say, 'In 'Numbers xii, 2, we read, 'Hath "'the Lord *only spoken* by Moses? "'hath He not spoken also by us?' 'According to some of my cor- 'respondents, and to Mr. Moon's 'pamphlet, this ought to be 'Hath "'the Lord spoken *only by Moses?*' 'I 'venture to prefer very much the 'words as they stand'. Now, strange as it may appear, after your assertion, it is nevertheless a fact that the words, as you quote them, do *not* occur either in the authorised version, known as King James's Bible of 1611, or in our present version,

THE DEAN'S ENGLISH.

or in any other version that I have ever seen; and the words, in the order in which you say I and your other correspondents would have written them, do occur *in every copy of the Scriptures to which I have referred!* So you very much prefer the words as they stand, do you? Ha! Ha! Ha! *So do I.* When next you write about the adverb '*only*', be sure you quote *only* the right passage of Scripture to suit your purpose."—p. 73.

THE QUEEN'S ENGLISH.

The Dean found another passage, which suited his purpose, and he quoted it.—p. 143.

XXVI.

"You say, 'Though some of the 'European rulers may be females, '*when spoken of altogether*, they may 'be correctly classified under the de-'nomination 'kings''. In this sentence, the clause which I have put in italics has, what our Gallic neighbours designate, 'a squinting 'construction', it looks two ways at once; that is, it may be construed as relating either to the words which precede, or to those which follow. Absurd as would be the sentence, its construction is such,

"Though some of the European rulers may be females, they may be correctly classified, when spoken of altogether, under the denomination 'kings'".—p. 97.

THE DEAN'S ENGLISH.	THE QUEEN'S ENGLISH.
that we may understand you to say, 'Some of the European rulers may 'be females, when spoken of al-'together.'"—p. 100.	

XXVII.

"You say, '*The derivation of the* '*word, as well as the usage of the* '*great majority of English writers,* '*fix the spelling the other way*'. *i.e.* *This* (as well as that) *fix it!* Excuse me, but I must ask you why you write thus, even though by putting the question, I put you '*in a fix*' to answer it."—p. 104.	"The derivation of the word, as well as the usage of the great majority of English writers, *fixes* the spelling the other way."—p. 33.

XXVIII.

"'At last we *abated* the nuisance 'by enacting, that in future the '*debatable* first syllable should be 'dropped'"—p. 106.	"At last we abated the nuisance by enacting that in future the first syllable should be dropped." —p. 56.

In conclusion, allow me, Dr. Alford, to thank you for the compliment which you unintentionally pay me in making the foregoing alterations. It must be admitted that you were wise to alter your sentences ;—to turn your words right and

K

left, in observance of certain rules. Forgive me if I smile at your quietly doing so after you had advised your readers to do nothing of the sort. It would have been more noble openly to acknowledge yourself to have been in error.

I now close this controversy, and take my leave of you; and, in doing so, I venture to express a hope that you will never again so presume upon your reputation and position as to treat an adversary with contempt. Few persons are so exalted that they can with safety be supercilious; few are so lowly that they may with impunity be despised.

I am, Rev. Sir,

Yours most respectfully,

G. WASHINGTON MOON.

To The Very Rev. Henry Alford, D.D.,
    Dean of Canterbury.

THE DEAN'S ENGLISH:

CRITICISM No. V.

PARALLELISMS.

REV. SIR,

It was not my intention to say anything more to you respecting the Queen's English; but happening one day to be passing a shop where second-hand books are sold, and seeing one with a perfectly plain cover, without any title, I had the curiosity to stop and open it. Finding that it was an old Quarterly Review containing an essay on '*Modern English*', I purchased it for sixpence; and I cannot resist the temptation to communicate to you what I then discovered; namely, the very close resemblance which parts of that essay bear to certain parts of your '*Queen's English*'. I looked for the date of the Review, to see if the writer had been borrowing from your book, without acknowledgment; but I found that the essay had been published some years before your book was in print. That you yourself are not the author of that essay is evident, not only from the fluency of style in which it is written, but also from the extensive knowledge which the author has of his subject.

With regard to literary parallelisms generally, I can believe it to be possible that to different students engaged in the same inquiry there will sometimes be presented the same ideas; but when, in two wholly independent works, those ideas are expressed in similar words, and are illustrated by the same examples; and when this occurs not once only, nor twice only, but nearly a score of times in a dozen pages, the coincidence is so singular that it challenges investigation. Are we to accept such facts as an astonishing instance of unintentional identity of thought and illustration in two writers; or are we to believe that the later writer has been too proud to acknowledge his obligations to the earlier, though not too proud to appropriate, and give forth as his own, the reflections and observations to which only the earlier writer could lay claim?

I purpose to bring together various passages from

'*Modern English*' and from '*The Queen's English*', and to ask you if you can give any explanation of the strange oneness of ideas observable in the two works; for although some of the parallelisms, considered separately, may be thought to be not very striking; as a whole, they are, beyond dispute, remarkable. That this opinion is not held by me only, will be apparent from the following quotation from '*The Saturday Review*'.—

"There is such a striking likeness between many
"of the Dean's remarks and illustrations and some
"which have appeared in our own pages, that we
"can hardly speak a good word for Dean Alford
"without at the same time speaking it for ourselves.
"To be sure we do not stand alone in this incidental
"likeness. We think we could point to an article
"in a Quarterly Review which has since 'ceased to
"'exist', the likeness between which and Dean
"Alford's '*Plea*' is more striking still." Need I tell you that the book which I purchased, and that to which the foregoing quotation refers, is the last number that was published of '*Bentley's Quarterly 'Review*'? Very few copies are now to be met with; but perhaps the author of '*Modern English*' will be induced to issue a reprint of that excellent essay. It ought to be read by every student of

the language. Whether its re-appearance would, by you personally, be regarded with pleasure, or not, of course I cannot doubt. Seeing that it has never yet come under your notice, you will be thankful to have the opportunity of carefully studying it; for, the author's thoughts and illustrations are so remarkably in unison with your own, that their oneness will often be a subject of mystery, even to the psychologist; while their parallel expressions will make another treasure to be added to the curiosities of literature. As for supposing that you could ever have been guilty of wilful plagiarisms, the idea is simply absurd. It is true that 'The Athenæum' says you owe to De Wette and Meyer the best part of your Commentary on the New Testament, and adds,—"*How closely De Wette is followed may be seen by comparing Alford's note on the Epistle to the Romans, ix. 12, 13, with that of the former, where the translation from the German is almost literal. In like manner,*" the reviewer continues, "*we could produce abundant proof that the Dean's 'I' is simply Meyer, or somebody else not named.*" It is true also that Tischendorf says of you,—"*Editionem meam recentissimam omni modo, neque vero sine malâ fide, suam in rem convertit.*"

Happily, however, the world knows, quite as well as you and I know, that the thoughts were all originally yours. By what means they came into the possession of those earlier writers is a mystery which they could best explain; but that they should have had the effrontery to publish those thoughts as their own, and never acknowledge themselves, even in the least degree, indebted to you for them, and that you should, moreover, be charged with being the plagiarist is, I can well conceive, enough to rouse your indignation, cause both your ears—I beg pardon, your "auricular appendages"—to tingle, and make even your "shovel hat", of which you speak, ruffle its beaver with anger, and curl up its brim in disdain.

I am, Rev. Sir,

Yours most respectfully,

G. WASHINGTON MOON.

Dis-je quelque chose d'assez belle ?—
L'Antiquité, toute en cervelle,
Prétend l'avoir dit avant moi :
C'est une plaisante donzelle !
Que ne venait-elle après moi ?
J'aurais dit la chose avant elle.

Le Chevalier de Cailly.

EXTRACTS FROM
'MODERN ENGLISH',

AN ESSAY IN

'BENTLEY'S QUARTERLY REVIEW', VOL. II. p. 518-542.

LEARNING to read is said to be the hardest of human acquirements. Nothing, indeed, could make us doubt the truth of the saying, except that so many people who succeed in mastering this greatest of difficulties break down in attempting the easier branches of knowledge which follow. To judge by experience, the hardest and rarest of all these later achievements would seem to be that of writing one's mother tongue. In these days, to be sure, everybody writes. But when we have got thus far, a fearful thought comes in,—How do we write? We all write English, but what sort of English? Can our sentences be construed? Do our words really mean what we wish them to? Of the vast mass of English which is written and printed, how much is really clear and straightforward, free alike from pedantry, from affectation, and from vulgarity?—*Modern English*, p. 518.

Of the many lines of thought which the prevalent

vices of style open to us, there is one which we wish to work out at rather greater length. It is that which relates to language in the strictest sense—to the choice of words. The good old Macedonian rule of calling a spade a spade finds but few followers among us. The one great rule of the 'high-polite style' is to call a spade anything but a spade.—*Modern English*, p. 525.

> Call a spade a spade, not *a well-known oblong instrument of manual husbandry.—Queen's English*, p. 278.

The shrinking from the plain honest speech of our Teutonic forefathers is ludicrous beyond everything. A public officer, from a prime minister to a post-office clerk, would be ashamed to send forth a despatch which a Dane, a German, or a Dutchman would recognize as written in a speech akin to his mother tongue.—*Modern English*, p. 526.

What are the rules we ought to follow in the choice of words? They seem to us to be very simple. Speak or write plain straightforward English, avoiding the affectation of slang or of technicality on the one hand, and the affectation of purism and archaic diction on the other. The history of our mixed language seems to furnish us with two very sound principles: *Never use a Romance word when a Teutonic one will do as well;—Modern English*, p. 529.

> *Never use a long word where a short one will do.—Queen's English, p.* 278.*

but on the other hand, *Never scruple to use a Romance word when the Teutonic word will not do so well.*

---

* The Dean, with his usual inconsistency, speaks in a recent number of 'The Contemporary Review' [Vol. I, p. 438] of a "chrononhotonthologos" of hymns. Poor wretched, lumbago-stricken beast of a word! Every joint in its long back groans out "*O!*"

As Sir Walter Scott, and so many after him, remarked, we still have to go to the Norman for our dressed meats. —*Modern English*, p. 531.

> We all remember that Gurth and Wamba complain in 'Ivanhoe' that the farm animals, as long as they [? the farm animals] had the toil of tending them [? Gurth and Wamba] were called by the Saxon and British names, *ox, sheep, calf, pig;* but when they were cooked and brought to table, their invaders [? the invaders of the pigs] enjoyed them under Norman and Latin names.—*Queen's English*, p. 243.

Our language is one essentially Teutonic; the whole skeleton of it is thoroughly so; all its grammatical forms, all the pronouns, particles, &c., without which a sentence cannot be put together; all the most necessary nouns and verbs, the names of the commonest objects, the expressions of the simplest emotions are still identical with that old mother-tongue whose varying forms lived on the lips of Arminius and of Hengist, &c.—*Modern English*, p. 529.

> Almost all its older and simpler ideas, both for things and acts, are expressed by Saxon words.—*Queen's English*, p. 242.

But the moment you get upon anything in the least degree abstract or technical, you cannot write a sentence without using Romance words in every line.—*Modern English*, p. 530.

> All its vehicles of abstract thought and science were clothed in a Latin garb.—*Queen's English*, p. 243.

We have the two elements, the original stock and the infusion; we must be content to use both; the only thing is to learn to use each in its proper place.—*Modern English*, p. 530.

> It would be mere folly in a man to attempt to confine himself to one or other of these main branches of the language.—*Queen's English*, p. 243.

The whole literature of notices, advertisements, and handbills—no small portion of our reading in these days—seems to have declared war to the knife against every trace of the Angles, Saxons, and Jutes.—*Modern English*, p. 527.

> Our journals seem indeed determined to banish our common Saxon words altogether.—*Queen's English*, p. 245.

There are a few words which will obstinately stick to their places: '*of*' and '*and*' '*in*' and '*out*', '*you*', '*I*', and '*they*', '*is*' and '*was*' and '*shall*', and a few more of the like kind, seem to have made up their minds not to move. But '*man*', '*woman*', '*child*', and '*house*' have already become something like archaisms.—*Modern English*, p. 527.

> You never read in them of a *man*, or a *woman*, or a *child*.—*Queen's English*, p. 245.

What *ens rationis* of any spirit would put up with being called '*a man*', when he can add four more syllables to his account of himself, and be spoken of as '*an individual*'? The *man* is clean gone, quite wiped out; his place is filled up by '*individuals*', '*gentlemen*', '*characters*', and '*parties*'.—*Modern English*, p. 527.

> A '*man*' is an '*individual*', or a '*person*', or a '*party*'.—*Queen's English*, p. 245.

The '*woman*', who in times past was the '*man's*' wife, has vanished still more completely. In all 'high-polite' writing, it is a case of 'Oh no, we never mention her.' The law of euphemisms is somewhat capricious; one cannot always tell which words are decent and which are not. The '*cow*' may be spoken of with perfect propriety in the most refined circles: in this case it is the male animal which is not fit to be mentioned; at least, American delicacy requires that he should be spoken of as a '*gentleman cow*'. But the female of '*horse*' is doubtful, that of '*dog*' is wholly proscribed. When the existence of such a creature must be hinted at, '*lady dog*' supplies a parallel formula to '*gentleman cow*'. And it really seems as if the old-fashioned feminine of '*man*' were fast getting proscribed in like manner.

We, undiscerning male creatures that we are, might have thought that '*woman*' was a more elegant and more distinctive title than '*female*'.—*Modern English*, p. 527.

> A '*woman*'. is a '*female*'.—*Queen's English*, p. 246.

We read only the other day a report of a lecture on the poet Crabbe, in which she who was afterwards Mrs. Crabbe was spoken of as '*a female to whom he had formed ' an attachment*'. To us, indeed, it seems that a man's wife should be spoken of in some way which is not equally applicable to a ewe lamb or to a favourite mare.—*Modern English*, p. 527.

> Why should a '*woman*' be degraded from her position as a rational being, and be expressed [*sic*] by a word which might belong to any animal tribe?—*Queen's English*, p. 246.

But it was a '*female*' who delivered the lecture, and we suppose the '*females*' know best about their own affairs. It is true, '*female*' is not our only choice: there are also '*ladies*' in abundance, and a still more remarkable class of '*young persons*'. Why a '*young person*' invariably means a young *woman* is a great mystery, especially as we believe an '*old person*' may be of either sex.—*Modern English*, p. 527.

A '*woman*' is, if unmarried, a '*young person*', which expression, in the newspapers, is always of the *feminine* gender.—*Queen's English.* p. 246.

Men and women being no more, it is only natural that '*children*' should follow them. There are no longer any '*boys*' and '*girls*'; there are instead '*young gentlemen*', '*young ladies*', '*juveniles*', '*juvenile members of the community*'.—*Modern English*, p. 527.

A '*child*' is a '*juvenile*'.—*Queen's English*, p. 246.

'*Houses*', too, have disappeared along with those who used to live in them. A '*man*' and a '*woman*' used to '*live*' in a '*house*'; but an '*individual*', or a '*party*', when he has conducted to the '*hymeneal altar*' the young '*female*', to whom he has '*formed an attachment*', cannot possibly do less than take her to '*reside*' in a '*residence*'. A '*house*'! there is no such thing: there is the genus '*residence*', divided into the several species of '*mansion*', '*villa residence*', '*cottage residence*', and '*tenement*'.—*Modern English*, p. 528.

A man going home is set down as '*an individual*' proceeding to his '*residence*'.—*Queen's English*, p. 248.

England used to be studded with '*inns*'—inns where it was said that one used to get one's warmest welcome. Now, there are no such things: to be sure, there are '*hotels*', which do not contain a single '*room*', but which are full of '*apartments*'.—*Modern English*, p. 528.

No one lives in '*rooms*' but always in '*apartments*'.—*Queen's English*, p. 248.

As man and his dwelling-place exist no longer, it is no wonder that all the sorts and conditions of men to whom one was used are now to be traced no longer. '*Lords*' and '*nobles*' have made way for an '*aristocracy*' of whom the law of England knows nothing; and the whole commons of this realm, who once were '*the people of* '*England*,' have now sunk into '*the million*', and '*the* '*masses*'. A '*shop*' is an '*establishment*'; and to '*take a walk*' is to '*promenade*'. Our '*landowners*' are '*pro-* '*prietors*', our '*farmers*' and '*yeomen*' are '*agriculturists*', and the '*working man*', who toils in the sweat of his brow, is content to cease to have a substantive being at all, and to be spoken of, like a metaphysical abstraction, as an '*operative*'.—*Modern English*, p. 528.

One form of the vice of which we complain is the fashion of using purely abstract nouns, just because they are longer and stranger, to express very simple things. '*Locality*', for instance, is a good philosophical term, but it is an intolerable barbarism when used as a mere synonym for '*place*'.—*Modern English*, p. 528.

> We never hear of a '*place*', it is always a '*locality*'.— *Queen's English*, p. 248.

'*Celebrity*', again, may pass as an abstract term; it is a mere vulgarism when used of a celebrated person. Then, again, there is the mere affectation of grandeur which makes a maid-of-all-work talk of her '*situation*', a house-agent talk of his '*clients*', and a schoolmaster dub himself '*Principal of a Collegiate Institution*'. In short, this sort of slang pursues us from our cradles to our graves. The unfortunate '*party*' or '*individual*', when at last he is removed from his earthly '*residence*', cannot, like his fathers, be '*buried*' in a '*church-yard*' or '*burying-ground*'; some '*company*' with '*Limited Lia-* '*bility*' is ready to '*inter*' him in a '*cemetery*' or in a '*metropolitan necropolis*'.—*Modern English*, p. 538.

Let us take another word used nearly like '*indi-* '*vidual*', though its use is, what that of '*individual*', we fear, hardly is, still felt as distinctively a vulgarism. This is '*party*'. Here is a technical term, thoroughly good in its proper place, abused into a vile piece of slang. —*Modern English*, p. 537.

> The word '*party*' for a man is especially offensive.—*Queen's English*, p. 246.

There is something very like it in our version of the Book of Tobit, vi, 7. 'We must make a smoke thereof 'before the man or the woman, and *the party* shall be no 'more vexed'.—*Modern English*, p. 537.

> Strange to say, the use is not altogether modern. It occurs in the English version of the apocryphal book of Tobit, vi, 7. 'If [a devil or] an evil spirit trouble any, one [? we] 'must make a smoke thereof before the man or the woman, 'and the *party* shall be no more vexed'.—*Queen's English*, p. 246.*

A witness, we remember, in the famous Waterloo Bridge and carpet-bag mystery, 'saw a *short party* go 'over the bridge'. A '*short party*', if it meant anything, might mean a political leader with a small following. But the witness hardly meant that he saw three or four statesmen of peculiar views go over the bridge, inasmuch as the '*short party*', if we rightly remember, turned out to be one woman.—*Modern English*, p. 537.

> Curious is the idea raised in one's mind by hearing of a *short party* going over the bridge.—*Queen's English*, p. 247.

---

* The reader will perceive that the Dean, by quoting only a *part* of the previous clause in the verse, has, virtually, misquoted the passage. According to the Dean's version, a smoke is to be made *of the evil spirit!* If that be so, might not Mrs. Glass's advice be useful?—" *First catch your hare* ". The Dean makes nonsense of the words; the verse really runs thus;—" And he said unto him, Touching the heart and the liver, if " a devil or an evil spirit trouble any, we must make a smoke thereof" —&c. G. W. M.

So much for nouns, we will now try a verb or two. No word can be better in its place than to '*inquire*', but it is a strange abuse of language to employ it when you simply mean to '*ask*'. Ask a waiter—waiters are, beyond all doubt, the greatest masters of the 'high-polite style'— any sort of question, the time of a train, or the chance of a dinner, and he always answers '*I'll inquire*'. Now, in the English language, to '*inquire*' implies a much more formal and lengthy business than merely to '*ask*'. A Commission, say at Wakefield or at Gloucester, '*in-quires*' into something, and, in the course of so doing, '*asks*' a great many particular questions. But in the other cases, if you use '*inquire*' indiscriminately for '*ask*', you destroy its special force in its proper place.— *Modern English*, p. 538.*

'*Inquire*', however, is harmless compared with another verb, whose abuse is one of the most marked signs of the style we complain of. Those who call '*men*' '*indivi-duals*' are sure to '*allude to*' them instead of speaking of them. Here, again, a thoroughly good word is perverted. To '*allude to*' a thing is to speak of it darkly,

* If the Dean, instead of wasting his time in a fruitless attempt to teach English, had turned his attention to the study of Hebrew, of which he is confessedly ignorant notwithstanding that as "a dignitary of "the church" he is "set for the defence of the gospel" and therefore ought to be "throughly furnished unto all good works", he would have been able to render good service to the cause of truth by demonstrating that the alleged contradiction between 1 Samuel xxviii, 6, and 1 Chronicles x, 14, is apparent only, and not real. The words which in those two passages are translated "*inquired*" are, in the original, very different, the one from the other. There is no contradiction. Saul *asked*, but he did not *inquire*, and therefore "*the Lord answered him not*". An important lesson, quite worthy of a Dean's teaching, is treasured in the apparent incongruity,—"*he inquired*", and yet, "*he inquired not*." "Ye "shall seek Me, and find Me, when ye shall search for Me with all your "heart.' G. W. M.

to hint at it without any direct mention. To use it in any other way is to lose the use of a good word in its proper place. But suppose a letter goes wrong in the Post-office, and you write to St. Martin's-le-Grand to complain. The invariable beginning of the official reply is to tell you the fate of the letter you *allude to* in your letter of such a date, though you have most likely *alluded to* nothing, but have told your story straightforwardly without hint or 'innuendo' of any kind.—*Modern English'*, p. 539.

> '*Allude to*' is used in a new sense by our journals, and not only by them, but also by the Government Offices. If I have to complain to the Post Office that a letter legibly directed to me at Canterbury has been missent to Caermarthen I get a regular red-tape reply, beginning ' The letter *allude*d to by you '. Now I did not '*allude to*' the letter at all; I mentioned it as plainly as I could.—*Queen's English*, p. 253.

We have now done. If the English language goes to the dogs, it will not be for want of our feeble protest. *We believe that to preserve our mother-tongue in its purity is a real duty laid upon every man who is called upon to speak or to write it.* We do not at all write in the interest of any sort of archaism or affectation. We ask only for pure and straightforward English, rejecting neither element of our mixed language, but using the words supplied by both, in their proper places and in their proper meaning. We ask for English free from all trace of the cant and slang of this or that school or clique or profession; for a language neither 'provincial' nor 'metropolitan'—English which is at once intelligible to the unlearned, and which will yet endure the searching criticism of the scholar.—*Modern English*, p. 542.

The New York '*Round Table*', in commenting on the foregoing passages, says:—

"The Dean, as far as we know, has made no public response to Mr. Moon's parallelisms. There appears, however, in '*The Contemporary Review*,' of which he is editor, a criticism upon '*Elijah the Prophet*', Mr. Moon's poem, of which we recently spoke as being in its third edition, the tone of which criticism is such as to make it capable of an interpretation very discreditable to Dean Alford, whose reputation in the course of the controversy has suffered not only in point of scholarship. '*The Imperial Review*' says of the poem:—

"'The metre adopted is that of the Spenserian stanza, with some slight alteration. With the exception of Lord Byron, no imitator of Spenser has shown a freedom and vigour in the handling of this graceful but difficult measure, that can be compared with the mastery almost universally evinced by Mr. Moon. . . . Taken as a whole, it is by far the best poem, on a sacred subject, that has appeared for a considerable time.'

"A further quotation from '*The Imperial Review*', though somewhat long, will show the nature of what it is to be hoped will not constitute the Dean's only reply in the plagiary matter."

Instead of giving the quotation referred to, I append the following letter, which embraces all that the critique contained, *and something additional.*

G. WASHINGTON MOON.

THE CAT'S PAW.

To the Editor of 'The Imperial Review.'

Sir,

A man who voluntarily enters upon the profession of arms is not one who thinks much of a few slight wounds. This is as true of him whose weapon is the pen, as of him whose weapon is the sword; I therefore have confidence that my motives in writing this letter will not be misinterpreted. I am proud to engage in combat with a foeman worthy of my steel; I delight in a wordy warfare with one who wields his weapon well; but I despise from my very soul the man who, under the pretext of doing battle for the truth, stabs at his opponent with a lie.

Honest criticism has a real value to an author. Even when it is unfavourable to the sale of his works, it may impart knowledge which will be serviceable to him in future studies. Believing this, I sent a copy of my poem, '*Elijah the Prophet*', to my old adversary, the Dean, editor of '*The Contemporary Review.*' I said to myself, 'Surely, if any person will be inclined to point out the 'errors in my composition, as far as he is able, it is he 'whose own compositions I have so severely criticised.' However, no notice of the poem appeared in '*The Contemporary Review*' during the sale of the first edition. At the end of six months a second edition was published, of which also a copy was sent to the editor. In six months more a third edition was published, of which I was about to send a copy, when I discovered in '*The Contemporary Review*' a notice of the poem, signed by the Rev. H. R. Haweis. I presume that the article was written at the Dean's request; it certainly met with his approval, or it would not have been inserted in the Review, of which he is editor.. The composition of much of the critique is wretched indeed; many of the sentences are as unconnected as a schoolboy's. But my object just now is not the exposure of the inelegancies of the language, but the condemnation of the utter untruthfulness of many of the assertions respecting the poem, and respecting the sacred Scriptures.

First, I am charged with being "*irreverent to a degree.*" Whether a little degree or a great degree is meant, this master of the Queen's English does not say. That the poem is irreverent towards fawning sycophants I frankly admit; but that it contains one irreverent thought or word concerning God I emphatically deny; and I call upon the Dean and his friend either to substantiate the charge, or publicly to acknowledge its injustice.

The reviewer says,—"*The prayer for rain on Carmel,* "*so thrilling and solemn with intense emotion, the great* "*scene of the Baal altars, the wonderful vision in the rock,* "*the fiery chariot—all is degraded.*" Now, there is not one word of prayer for rain on Carmel on record in the whole of the Bible. Judge then of this clergyman's truthfulness in describing it as being "*so thrilling and solemn* "*with intense emotion*"! St. James tells us that Elijah prayed for rain; but where he prayed, and in what language he prayed, we are not told; therefore, to state that I have degraded "*the prayer for rain on Carmel, so thrill-* "*ing and solemn with intense emotion*", is to state what is utterly false; for as there is no prayer for rain on Carmel to be found in the Bible, so neither is there in my poem.

To proceed:—"*The great scene of the Baal altars.*" Here is another instance of this clergyman's ignorance of that Book which ought to have been the study of his life! It would seem that the facts of Scripture are so jumbled together in his mind that he has actually confounded the sacrifice offered by Baal's worshippers on Mount Carmel, with the sacrifices offered by Balaam on the high places of Baal, near the plains of Moab! In no other manner can I account for the gross error in the foregoing quotation. By reference to 1 Kings xviii, 26, it will be found that there was but one Baal altar on Mount Carmel. Therefore, to say that I have degraded "*the great scene of the Baal altars,*" is to say that I have degraded that concerning which I have not written one word. See Numbers xxii, 41, and xxiii, 1.

"*The wonderful vision in the rock.*" Worse and worse! There is not anywhere in the history of Elijah a single sentence about a vision in a rock. Here, as elsewhere, this would-be learned divine has confounded characters and incidents which have not the slightest connexion with each other. In the preceding clause the prophet Elijah was confounded with the prophet Balaam; in this clause he is confounded with the great lawgiver, Moses. It was he, and not Elijah, who had the wonderful vision in the rock, as may be seen by a glance at Exodus xxxiii, 22. Moses had said to God,—"*I beseech Thee, show me* "*Thy glory*"; and God, in His gracious reply, answered, "*It shall come to pass, while My glory passeth by, that I* "*will put thee in a cleft of the rock.*" When, on the same mountain, the Lord passed before Elijah, after the great and strong wind, and the earthquake, fire, and still small voice had heralded his coming, Elijah, unlike Moses, who was hid in a cleft of the rock, had, by divine command, gone forth from the cave and stood upon the mount. See 1 Kings xix, 11—13.

The next clause is, "*the fiery chariot—all is degraded.*" The reader shall judge for himself of the justice of this remark. This is the way in which I have "*degraded*"

THE FIERY CHARIOT.

The sun had set; and, as they journeyed on,
They thought they caught the sound of distant thunder;
Then nearer, clearer; but, o'erhead, stars shone;
And, on the horizon, silv'ry clouds sailed under
The deep blue sky. With mingled awe and wonder,
The prophets turned and saw that towards them came
From heav'n a chariot and steeds of flame!
While Nebo's sacred mountain, with age hoary
And crowned with snow, was radiant with the glow
Of that celestial and unutterable glory.

Ethereal, yet visible; for, bright
Unto intensity through purest light
Indwelling, was that chariot of the skies.
The horses, too, were creatures not of earth;
Their necks were clothed with thunder; and their eyes,
Starry with beauty, told of Heav'nly birth.
No harness fettered them; no curb nor girth
Restrained the freedom of those glorious ones,
Nor traces yoked the chariot at their heels;
It followed them, as planets follow suns
Through trackless space, in their empyreal courses;
For lo! the fiery spirit of the horses
Was as a mighty presence in the wheels,
And in the dazzling whirlwind which behind them flew
And caught Elijah up, as sunlight drinks the dew.

Away, away to Heav'n those steeds upbore him;
Leaving the clouds as dust beneath their feet.

> Wide open flashed the golden gates before him;
> And angel-forms of splendour rose to greet
> The favoured prophet. Oh! the rapture sweet!
> The ecstasy most thrilling which came o'er him!—
> But thoughts are voiceless when we soar thus high;
> And, like the lark that vainly strives to beat
> With little wings the air and pierce the sky,
> We fall again to earth. Elisha there
> Wept o'er his loss, but wept not in despair.
> No; though a few regretful tear-drops fell,
> He knew that with Elijah all was well;
> For through the open gates of Heav'n there rang
> Strains of the song of welcome which the angels sang.
>
> O who can picture that transcendent sight!
> Who fitly can relate the wondrous story!
> Who paint the aërial beauty of that night,
> Or sing the fleetness of those steeds of glory
> And God's triumphant chariot of light
> Entering Heav'n! Never, in depth or height,
> Had mortal gazed on such a scene before:
> Never shall years, how long soe'er their flight,
> The solemn grandeur of that hour restore,
> Till Heav'n's last thunder peals forth "It is done!"
> And the archangel, dazzling as the sun,
> Descends to earth; and, standing on the shore
> Of ages, swears with upraised hand by ONE
> Who lived ere time its cycles had begun,
> That time shall be no more.

As the Dean lays claim to being a poet as well as a critic, I challenge him to compose and publish a poetical description of the translation of Elijah, which shall be less *degrading* than is the one which he has so unscrupulously condemned.

We now come to a beautiful specimen of criticism. It is the concluding sentence in the review; and is doubtless regarded with great satisfaction by the writers. I read :—" *But Mr. Moon has neither the spiritual insight of a Robertson, nor the intuitive art* [' intuitive art' ! I suppose that we shall hear next of acquired instinct] *of a Mendelssohn, therefore* [mark the logic of the sequence] *his prayer for rain* [I have already remarked that there is not, in the history of Elijah, any language of prayer for rain, either in the Bible or in my poem] *is feeble rhodomontade*, [the dunce does not know even how to spell! He is evidently ignorant of the fact that the word takes its origin from one of Boyardo's heroes, *Rodomonte,* a king of Algiers. See ' Notes and Queries ', 4th series, vol. iii, p. 379.] *his great sacrifice nothing but a sham gone through by unimpassioned mimes, his vision in the rock a tedious dialogue* [how can a vision be a dialogue?] *accompanied by stage lightning* [as for the "stage lightning," the following are my words :—

> An earthquake shook Mount Horeb to its base ;
> Fires subterranean then finding vent,
> Their flames shot up to heav'n, as if to trace
> Jehovah's awful name upon unbounded space.]

" *his fiery steeds the property of some stage manager* [vide seq.] *and Elijah himself little more than a magnified conjuror.*" Judge of this clergyman's honesty of representation. This is my description of Elijah :—

> The brightest jewel in the costliest shrines
> Where God is worshipped is humility.
> 'Tis like a star which trembles while it shines ;
> And, through its trembling, brighter seems to be.—
> That jewel, in its purest brilliancy,
> Adorned Elijah's character.—With men,
> He was a man !—and bowed to none ! But he,
> Before Jehovah,—was a child ; and when
> He thought of all God's love to him, he wept again.

'*A magnified conjuror*'! It has been well said that a man's language is generally a very good indication of his habits of thought and of action. If we hear a person speak of his friend's peculiarities "cropping out", we naturally judge that the speaker has recently been studying geology. If a man speaks of the "tone and colour" of a discourse, we at once conclude that he is an artist. The boy who, returning from an errand, apologized for the long time that he had been absent, by saying, that he had had to open "a whole folio" of doors to get at that which he sought, told very plainly the nature of his occupation; and when, in the criticism under review, the writer speaks of Jezebel as preparing to "*throw her last "die"*, and illustrates some of his remarks by references to "*conjurors*", "*mimes*", "*stage lightning*", and "*stage "managers*", we draw our own inferences as to the circumstances which have made these matters so familiar to a clergyman. The Rev. H. R. Haweis would be acting in a manner far more befitting his character, or at least his profession, were he to manifest less familiarity with the language of gaming-tables and theatres, and greater familiarity with the language of his Bible; and the Dean would show himself to be a wiser man, were he to give clearer evidence that in his estimation there is nothing so beautiful as truth.

     I am, Sir,
       Your obedient Servant,
         G. WASHINGTON MOON.

LONDON.

APPENDIX.

THE QUEEN'S ENGLISH.

A Criticism from 'The Churchman.'

WE scarcely know whether to look upon the labours of Dean Alford in the cause of our language as a loss or as a gain. In many ways his remarks on the Queen's English must have been attended with good results. The wide circulation which they obtained, when first published in '*Good Words*', has caused a vast number of persons to pay far more attention to this much-neglected subject than they had ever done before. Many have been brought for the first time to bestow a serious attention on their mother-tongue, and to see that the consideration of the words in which their thoughts are clothed is a matter of no small moment, and furnishes a true test of a nation's character and progress. In these papers they have been warned against the use of mean and slipshod English, against an affected and unnatural style, and, in fact, against most of the faults which mar the language of the present day, and which may be found so abundant in the columns of the periodical press, and in the conversation of half-educated persons. On the other hand, the Dean has set an evil example by rendering the standard of right and wrong in language more wavering and uncertain than ever: custom, according to him, is the only court of appeal, and the laws of grammar are to be left to pedants and pedagogues. If this is to be the case, it seems hopeless to bring many of those, who habitually break the laws of language, to a sense of their shortcomings. They have been brought up from their birth amongst persons who commit the same faults, and they are unable to see the nature of these faults. If referred to the laws of grammar, they appeal to the authority of Dean Alford to show that it is pedantic to be guided by grammarians; if referred to the custom of educated persons, they maintain their own experience against that of their reprovers, and declare that their own usage is the customary one, and that the one recommended to them is contrary to custom.

Amongst the paradoxical statements of Dean Alford, we have selected some of the most prominent for comment. At the time of the first appearance of these papers, a great, and, in our opinion, not unreasonable, outcry was made against the sanctioning of the phrase, "It is me". The Dean brings forth Dr. Latham in support of his opinion, and refers us to the following extract from that gentleman's *History of the English Language*:—

"We may.........call the word *me* a secondary nominative, inasmuch as such phrases as *It is me—It is I*, are common. To call such expressions incorrect English, is to assume the point. No one says that *c'est moi* is bad French, and *c'est je* is good. The fact is, that with us the whole question is a question of degree. Has or has not the custom been sufficiently prevalent to have transferred the forms *me*, *ye*, and *you*, from one case to another? Or perhaps we may say, is there any real custom at all in favour of *I*, except so far as the grammarians have made one? It is clear that the French analogy is against it. It is also clear that the personal pronoun as a predicate may be in a different analogy from the personal pronoun as a subject".

We have great respect for Dr. Latham's learning, but in a matter like the present we cannot submit to his authority. Modern writers on language, when treating of well-known words and phrases, are often apt to seek opportunities for displaying their own ingenuity in giving unusal explanations of them, and Dr. Latham is by no means free from a partiality for crotchets of this kind. There is no analogy between English and French in this matter. It is a peculiarity of the French language that each pair of words which represents the different cases of the singular personal pronouns in other languages is in French represented by three words instead of two. I, me—*je, me, moi;* thou, thee—*tu, te, toi;* he, him—*il, le, lui. Moi, toi, lui,* are used as nominative cases when coming after the verb. If Dr. Latham's reasoning is right, that because we have in French *c'est moi,* not *c'est je,* therefore, it is right to say in English, "it is me", not "it is I": then it follows that because we say *c'est toi,* not *c'est tu, c'est lui,* not *c'est il,* it is right to say "it is "thee", "it is him", or "her". It seems to us as bad grammar to say, "it is me", in English, as *c'est me* in French. He further says that "when constructions are "predicative, a change is what we must expect rather "than be surprised at" We see this change of construction in French when the pronouns are predicative, because each pronoun has three distinct forms, but as English, together with the rest of the European languages (with which we are acquainted), has only two forms of personal pronouns, therefore the change cannot take place when the construction is predicative. Another reason given by Dr. Latham for the usuage is, that *me* is not the proper, but only the adopted, accusative of *I,* "being in fact a distinct and independent form of the "personal pronoun". We do not see why, because *me* is the adopted accusative of *I*, it should become "a second-"ary nominative". All the European languages of which we have any knowledge have an adopted accusative for the first person singular, but we do not find in them any traces of its being used as a secondary nominative (though it may appear so in French); why, then, are we to grant this license to English, merely to gratify a careless habit which may easily be corrected? We now come to consider Dean Alford's own remarks on these three little words. He seems to think that the reason for the substitution of *me* for *I* is a shrinking from obtruding our own personality;* and endeavours to confirm his view by referring to an instance of the contrary practice in the well-known passage:—

"He said unto them, 'It is I, be not afraid'. This is a capital instance; for it shows us at once why the nominative should be sometimes used. The Majesty of the Speaker here, and his purpose of re-assuring the disciples by the assertion that it was none other than Himself, at once point out to us the case in which it would be proper for the nominative, and not the accusative, to be used".

---

* "This shrinking from the use of the personal pronoun, this authophoby, as it may be called, is not indeed a proof of the modesty it is designed to indicate; any more than the hydrophobia is a proof that there is no thirst in the constitution. *On the contrary, it rather betrays a morbidly sensitive self-consciousness.*"

"So far indeed is the anxiety to suppress the personal pronoun from being a sure criterion of humility, that there is frequently a ludicrous contrast between the conventional generality of our language and the egotism of the sentiments expressed in it."

"Modesty must dwell within, in the heart; and a brief *I* is the modestest, most natural, simplest word I can use." '*Guesses at Truth*,' pp. 142, 148, 150.

APPENDIX. 159

We will venture to say that the sole reason which the translators of the Bible had for writing "it is I" in this verse, was because they considered it the proper grammatical phrase, and "it is me" ungrammatical. How would Dean Alford account for the two following verses, Matt. xxvi. 22, 25, "And they were exceeding sorrowful, "and began every one of them to say unto Him, Lord, is "it I?" "Then Judas, which betrayed him, answered "and said, "Master, is it I?" Certainly, according to the Dean's reasoning, we ought in each case to have, "Is "it me?" but there is no trace of such a usage throughout the Bible.

Dean Alford asks the question, "What are we to think "of the question whether *than* does or does not govern "an accusative case?"—

"The fact is, that there are two ways of constructing a clause with a comparative and '*than*'. You may say either '*than I*' or '*than me*'. If you say the former, you use what is called an elliptical expression, *i.e.* an expression in which something is left out—and that something is the verb '*am*'. 'He is wiser than I', being filled out, would be, 'He is wiser than I am'. 'He is wiser than me' is the direct and complete construction"

We agree that there are two ways of constructing the clause—a right way and a wrong way. "He is wiser "than I" is right. "He is wiser than me" is wrong. There is no occasion to make use of an ellipse at all. *Than* is a conjunction, and, therefore, cannot govern an accusative case, as it is a fundamental rule of all languages that conjunctions should couple like cases. We cannot see in what way "He is wiser than me" can be more complete than "He is wiser than I". Again, we find the rule laid down by the Dean, that, when solemnity is required, the construction in the nominative is used;

and he quotes John xiv, 28, "My father is greater than I". This would be of some weight if he could bring a single instance in which *than* of itself governed an accusative in a case where solemnity was not required, but we do not think that he will find one in the Bible. In Gen. xxxix, 8, Joseph says to Potiphar's wife, "Behold, my master knoweth not what is with me in the house, and "he hath committed all that he hath to my hand; there "is none greater in the house than I; neither hath "he kept back", &c. We cannot suppose that the translators wished to represent Joseph as attaching any solemnity to the words "there is none greater than I", which are introduced in the middle of a long sentence. The reason for their occurring thus is because the translators knew that the phrase, "there is none greater than "me", is entirely ungrammatical. Dean Alford considers that the invariable use of "than whom", instead of "than "who", is a proof that *than* governs an accusative case, as in '*Paradise Lost*', ii. 299:—

"Which, when Beelzebub perceived, *than whom*,
"Satan except, none higher sat".

We quite agree that, to say "than who", would be intolerable in this instance to most ears, but we do not consider that this single anomalous expression is enough to warrant us in saying that "than" takes the accusative. The expressions "than whom", "than which", are very sparingly used in writing, and never in ordinary conversation. Probably the first person who wrote "than "whom", did so in ignorance of the rules of grammar, and the error was so perpetuated by his coypists that it became a settled usage. Another explanation of it is, that the "m" was added for the sake of euphony. However that may be, we cannot allow that one anomaly of this kind can justify us in going counter to the grammar and usage of all languages.

As is a word of precisely the same character as *than*: would Dean Alford defend the vulgarisms, "I am as tall "as him", "He is as tall as me"?*

A correspondent has kindly sent us a well-known example of the latter usage from one of our standard poets:—

> "The nations not so blest as *thee*
> "Must in their turn to tyrants fall,
> "Whilst thou shalt flourish, great and free,
> "The dread and envy of them all."
>
> THOMSON'S '*Rule Britannia.*'

In our opinion the first line of this stanza is utterly indefensible.

The Dean upholds the use of the verb "to leave", in a neuter, or, as he bids us term it, an absolute sense. He defends the sentence "I shall not *leave* before December 1" on the ground that the verb is still active, but the object is still suppressed. We deny that to "leave" is here used in an active sense; it is synonymous with "to "go away", "depart", &c., which are neuter verbs. The Dean brings forward the instances of the verbs "to read" and "to write", as if they were analogous cases because they may be used at will either transitively or intransitively. These verbs, however, themselves express an occupation, just as much as to run, to sit, or to stand. If we wish to know how any one is spending his time, it is a sufficient answer to say "He is reading"; if we are aware of that fact, and wish to know what is the object of his study, then we must use the verb transitively, and say, "He is reading '*The Queen's English*'", or any other

*Yes. See '*The Queen's English*', 2nd edition, page 160.—G. W. M.

M

book. "To read" has become to all of us a complete notion; "to leave" is not so; and, as we said before, must be used as an equivalent for to depart, or go away, in the phrase quoted. This is an unnecessary extension of its signification, and as all such extensions give rise to more or less ambiguity, they should be avoided. The use of a verb in an intransitive as well as a transitive sense must always be a matter depending entirely on authority. Such a use of "to leave" was ignored formerly, and has arisen only within comparatively few years from the carelessness of slipshod speakers and writers. In the present day it is eschewed by good writers of English; by others it is used invariably, but quite unnecessarily, in a neuter sense.

In Dr. Alford's objections to the restrictions placed by grammarians on the words *first* and *last*, *former* and *latter*, he makes the following remarks :—

"'*First*' is unavoidably used of that one in a series with which we begin, whatever be the number which follow; whether many or few. Why should not *last* be used of that one in a series with which we end, whatever be the number which preceeded, whether many or few?"

We should have thought that the answer was quite evident. *First* has two meanings; it stands for the superlative of the comparative *former*, and for the ordinal corresponding to the cardinal number *one*. *Last* is used only as the superlative of *latter*; it cannot, therefore, be ever used in numerical statements. In speaking of a book in two volumes, which are numbered 1 and 2, we refer to the 1st or the 2nd volume; but 1st is not here the same as *first*, the superlative of former. This is easily shown in the case of most of our large public schools, where the 6th form is the first, and the 1st form the last in the school. If we had such a word as *oneth* to stand as the ordinal of *one*, we should say that the sixth form is the first, and the oneth the last; as it is, we are obliged to make *first* do duty in each case.

We do not agree theoretically with the Dean's remarks on the aspiration of the "h" in *humble*, though practically we think it advisable to follow the growing usage of the day, and sound the "h". It was formerly almost as common to say *umble* as it is to say *onour* and *(h)our*. In regard to the words "*ospital*", "*erb*", and "*umble*", our author says that all of them are "very offensive, but the "last of them by far the worst, especially when heard "from officiating Clergymen". We believe that the reason why the Clergy have so commonly adopted the practice of sounding the "h" in *humble*, is because educated persons cannot endure the idea of its being said of them that they drop their "h's"; directly, therefore, the custom became prevalent of aspirating *humble*, the Clergy at once took it up. It will be the same as soon as it becomes at all usual to sound the "h" in honour, honesty, &c. We deny that "*umble* and *hearty* no man can "pronounce without a pain in his throat"; it is just as easy to pronounce as "*under heaven*".

There are many other remarks in this work with which we cannot agree, but we have no wish to weary our readers with further criticisms on this somewhat dry subject.

THE QUEEN'S ENGLISH.
A CRITICISM FROM ROUTLEDGE'S MAGAZINE.

THE study of language is one of the most instructive and, at the same time, one of the most interesting occupations with which we can employ ourselves; and, in the present age of advanced education, it is absolutely necessary for everybody to obtain a knowledge of his own language, and to read, speak, and write it in accordance with the known rules on the subject. However well taught a man may be in other branches of study, he will never make his way in the world unless he can speak correctly, since correct speaking is, as it were, the outward attribute of the gentleman, and the one by which his other qualifications are judged.

The Dean is evidently not a graceful writer of English, as he is sure to have put forth all his strength in the composition of a book on language. This strength, however, seems to consist in devising the most unnatural manner of writing good English, and in violating some of Lord Kames's most important rules with regard to words expressing things connected in thought being placed as near together as possible.

'*The Queen's English*,' we must state, professes to be a reprint from a widely circulated periodical entitled '*Good Words*,' and the subject is said to be 'presented to the public in a considerably altered form.'

This is strictly true, for, having compared the reprint with the original articles, we are able to compliment the Dean on the many judicious alterations he has made; thanks, perhaps, to the suggestions given by a gentleman styled, in a country paper, "a knight, bearing on "his shield the emblem of the lunar orb", and other lovers of pure English who have considered that the reverend grammarian has in some way defiled the pure well of English.

Sitting down with the book,* and the volume of '*Good Words*' for 1863 before us, we note no great difference

* Second Edition.

APPENDIX.

until we come to the following expression: "The Queen "is of course no more the proprietor of the English language *than you or I*"—(see '*Good Words*'), but in the volume we have "*than any one of us.*" Why this change? On page 152 of the book we read: "What are we to think "of the question, whether 'than' does or does not govern "an accusative case? 'than I': 'than me': which is "right? My readers will probably answer without hesita- "tion, the former. But is the latter so certainly wrong? "*We are accustomed to hear it stigmatized as being so;* "*but, I think, erroneously.* Milton writes, '*Paradise Lost,*' "ii, 299,—

"'Which when Beelzebub perceived, *than whom*,
Satan except, none higher sat.'

"And thus every one of us would speak: 'than who', "would be intolerable. *And this seems to settle the question.*"

So the Dean thinks. We, however, do not. Poetry is not often considered a high authority on matters of grammatical construction, although the Dean seems to think it should be, since this is the only instance of "than" governing the accusative that he deigns to cite: besides, it is evident that in many cases, the employment of the accusative instead of the nominative, gives to the sentence another meaning, thus:

1 He likes you better than me.
2 He likes you better than I.

Surely it is manifest to everybody that the first form means that he likes you better than [he likes] me, and that the latter means, he likes you better than I [like you]; and yet our Dean in an authoritative manner says, that you may say either "*than I*", or "*than me*", but that the former should be used only when solemnity is required, as "My Father is greater than I."

Is solemnity required when mention is made of the Queen in regard to her proprietorship of the English language? We trow not. Why, then, does our Dean lay down a rule, and break it on the first page of his Essays? This reflection seems to have occurred to the mind of the author, who probably in his reprint weighed with care every expression he made use of. This at any rate seems the only reason why he should alter "*than you or I*" to "*than any one of us*," and thus screen himself under an expression which fits either rule.

Let us pause for a short time and note what some authorities write about this conjunction. Lowth is of opinion that such forms as "thou art wiser than me" are bad grammar. Mr. E. F. Graham, in his excellent book on English style, quotes the objective case after "than" as a downright grammatical error, whilst our old friend Lindley Murray devotes a page and a half to the discussion of this question, and, after citing the lines of Milton just quoted, concludes his notice by saying, "The "phrase *than whom*, is, however, avoided by the best "modern writers". The crowning point of all, however, is that the very author whom Dean Alford quotes in support of his theory, says in the first book of '*Paradise* '*Lost*':—

"What matter where, if I be still the same.
And what I should be, all but less *than he*?"

Near the end of a paragraph in the first Essay occurs the following sentence, which is omitted in the book:— "And I really don't wish to be dull; so please, dear "reader, to try *and* not think me so."

It was wise, indeed, on the Dean's part, to omit this sentence in his book, for probably it contains the worst mistake he has made. Try *and* think, indeed! Try *to* think, we can understand. Fancy saying "the dear "reader *tries and thinks* me so"; for, mind, a conjunction is used only to connect words, and can govern no case at all. However, as the Dean has not allowed this to appear in his book, we refrain from alluding further to it.

As the Dean admits that his notes are for the most part insulated and unconnected, we presume that we need make no apology if our critical remarks happen to partake of the same character; for, the reader will easily understand that criticism on unconnected topics must itself also be unconnected.

Who does not recollect with pleasure those dear old ladies, Sairah Gamp and Betsey Prig? " *Which*, altering "the name to Sairah Gamp, I drink," said Mrs. Prig.

" As I write these lines, *which* I do while waiting in a "refreshment room at Reading between a Great Western "and a South Eastern train," says the Dean. It is always interesting to know the time when, and the place where, great men have written their books; and we thank Dean Alford for telling us where he wrote this elegant sentence; but fancy, what a very small refreshment room there must be at Reading, if it stands between two trains. May we venture to suggest that the sentence would have been improved if "which I do", and the words from "between" to "train", had been altogether omitted. "*Which* you are right, my dear ", says Mrs. Harris.

On page 67 the Dean comes to that which he says must form *a principal part* of his little work. The principal part means, we believe, more than half of anything, but as in the present work there are evidently two principal parts (at least), it appears that the volume contains more than the two halves. Perhaps the Dean was waiting between two trains in Ireland when he penned this sentence.

With regard to the demonstrative pronouns, "*this* "refers to the nearest person or thing, and *that* to the "most distant", says Murray. This, however, is not Dean Alford's view of the matter.

After mentioning the name Sophœnetus (and no other) he writes, "Every clergyman is, or ought to be, familiar "with his Greek Testament; two minutes' reference to "*that* will show him how every one of *these* names ought "to be pronounced."

Who is right here—Lindley Murray or the Dean of Canterbury? Stop! stop! Not so fast. In theory, the Dean agrees with our grammarian; for, eleven pages further on, he says,—"'*this*' and '*these*' refer to persons "and things present, or under immediate considera-"tion; '*that*' and '*those*' to persons and things not pre-"sent, nor under immediate consideration." He then mentions a Scottish friend, who always designates the book which he has in hand as "*that book*." Surely this Scotchman and the Dean belong to one family.

We now come with much pleasure to the last fault which we have to find with Dr. Alford's book. We have purposely deferred any mention of this particular subject until now, on the same principle as that which actuated the schoolboy who always kept the best till the last.

On page 280 we read the following excellent remarks:—
"Avoid, likewise, all *slang* words. There is no greater "nuisance in society than a talker of slang. It is only fit "(when innocent, which it seldom is) for raw schoolboys "and one-term freshmen, to astonish their sisters with."

Of course, after expressing himself so strongly on this point, it is not to be expected that, in a work on the *Queen's English*, Dean Alford will make use of slang terms. Let us see.

On page 2, he tells us, "He bowls along it with ease in "a vehicle, which a few centuries ago would have been "broken to pieces in a deep rut, or [would have] *come to* "*grief* in a bottomless swamp."

In the original notes the words "*would have*" were omitted. One of his censors then suggested that the sentence was "or *would have been* come to grief". On page 132 of his book, the Dean defends his elliptical mode of spelling: but, on page 2, by altering it, he tacitly admits that he is wrong.

On page 41 he tells us about some persons who had been detained by a *tipple*.

On page 178 we are told that the Dean and his family took a *trap* from the inn.

And, on page 154, he writes to Mr. Moon, "If you see "an old *party* in a shovel that will be me". Whereas, on page 245, in sneering at our journals he says, a man in them is a *party*. Now we are persuaded that no newspaper writes of a man in such vulgar language. This style seems to have been left to a Dean when writing on controversial subjects.

THE QUEEN'S ENGLISH.

A Criticism from 'The Patriot.'

DEAN ALFORD has collected into a book his papers contributed to '*Good Words*' and, of course, has subjected them to a fresh and final revision. He tells us, indeed, that "now, in a considerably altered form, they are pre-"sented to the public"; so that we may fairly regard both the canons and the composition of this volume as the deliberate and final setting forth of the Dean's notions of the proprieties of the English language. No plea of hasty writing, such as unfortunate newspaper writers, or public lecturers, or even magazine contributors, might fitly urge, is valid here. The Dean tells us, too—what we are very glad to learn, and what speaks well for the Christian placability of both parties—that the somewhat sharp passage of arms betwixt Mr. Moon and himself has ended in an invitation to dinner and a real friendship. "From antagonism we came to inter-"course; and one result of the controversy I cannot "regret—that it has enabled me to receive Mr. Moon as a "guest, and to regard him henceforward as my friend". Will this deprive the public of the benefit of Mr. Moon's criticisms upon the present volume? We should be sorry to think so; for there really is much to be said about it, and, we fear, much fault to be found with it. Dean Alford has rendered good service to his generation. He was an exemplary working clergyman; and he is, we doubt not, as exemplary a Dean. He is an excellent poet, and his beautiful hymn, "*Lo, the storms of life are break-"ing*", sung to sweet music, has often soothed our soul. We cannot call him an accomplished Greek scholar; but he has compiled the most useful working Greek Testament of our generation; amenable to a thousand adverse criticisms, but laboriously bringing together almost all that working clergymen need.

But with all this we cannot regard him as an authority on the philosophy of the English language, or as an example of its more accurate use. It is strange that men should imagine themselves to be that which they are so far from being, that they are unconscious even of their defects. Only a scholar of the widest philological reading and of the nicest discrimination should have presumed to write a book on the use and abuse of the

Queen's English. No doubt Dean Alford thinks that he is such a scholar, and that his composition, if not in his ordinary sermons, yet in this volume, is faultless. We regret to be compelled to think otherwise. His style, where not positively ungrammatical, is loose, and flabby, and awkward; his sentences are ungainly in construction, and sometimes positively ludicrous in the meaning which they involuntarily convey. We will take a few instances; and we begin with the third sentence in the book.

"It [the term "Queen's English"] is one rather familiar "and conventional, than strictly accurate". As Dean Alford uses it, the adverb "rather" qualifies the terms "familiar" and "conventional". He means it to qualify the term "strictly accurate", and should have said, "It is one familiar and conventional rather than strictly "accurate".

"For language wants all these processes, as well as "roads do", is scarcely as elegant as a critical Dean should have written.

Again: "And it is by processes of this kind in the "course of centuries, that our English tongue has been "ever adapted", &c.; instead of "It is by processes of "this kind that, in the course of centuries, our English "tongue", &c.

"Carefulness about minute accuracies of inflexion and "grammar may appear to some very contemptible". We trust that the Dean is not one of these; but would it not have been better to write, "may to some appear very "contemptible"?

"The other example is one familiar to you, of a more "solemn character": and what is it to those given to levity? The Dean meant to say, "The other example is "of a more solemn character, and is one familiar to you".

"The late Archdeacon Hare, in an article on English "orthography in the '*Philological Museum*'". We did not know that the English orthography of the '*Philolog-* '*ical Museum*' was peculiar, or needed an article. The Dean means "in an article in the '*Philological Museum*' "on English orthography".

".We do not follow rule in spelling the other words, "but custom". An elegant writer would have said, "In "spelling the other words we do not follow rule, but "custom".

These specimens occur in the first twelve pages; how many the entire volume would afford, is beyond our calculation.

With many of Dean Alford's canons, both of derivation and of pronunciation, and even of spelling, we have almost equal fault to find; but we forbear. We must say, however, that, notwithstanding Mr. Latham's authority, and at the risk of being reckoned "grammarians of the " smaller sort", we are still unconvinced of the propriety of saying, even colloquially, "It's me", and of the pedantry of saying, "It's I".

We must add, too, that a somewhat unseemly egotism and gossipiness pervades the book—pardonable enough in popular lectures, but surely to be excluded from a philological treatise. The Dean seems to have no plan, but just to say anything that comes first, and to say it anyhow. Perhaps he thinks the chit-chat of a Dean sufficient for all persons of less dignity.

Dean Alford, of course, says many just and useful things, and will, we trust, do something to correct some errors and vulgarisms. But it is one thing to read Dean Alford's sentences, and it is another to read Macaulay's.

THE DEAN'S ENGLISH *v.* THE QUEEN'S ENGLISH.

A CRITICISM FROM THE LONDON REVIEW.

A WRITER in the current number of '*The Edinburgh Review*' censures Mr. Moon for hypercritically objecting to sentences the meaning of which is perfectly clear, though it is possible, having regard to the mere construction, to interpret them in a sense ludicrously false. We think that Mr. Moon does occasionally exhibit an excessive particularity; but many of his criticisms on Dr. Alford are, *as the reviewer himself admits*, thoroughly deserved. Because certain ambiguities have become recognised forms of speech, and are universally understood in the correct sense, a writer is not entitled to indulge in a lax mode of expression, which a little trouble would have rendered unimpeachable without any sacrifice of ease, grace, or naturalness. The reviewer quotes, or imagines, two sentences to which no reasonable objection could be made, though the construction is assuredly not free from ambiguity:—" Jack was very "respectful to Tom, and always took off his hat when "he met him." "Jack was very rude to Tom, and "always knocked off his hat when he met him." Now, as a mere matter of syntax, it might be doubtful whether Jack did not show his respect to Tom by taking off Tom's hat, and his rudeness by knocking off his own; but the fault is hardly a fault of construction—it is a fault inherent in the language itself, which has not provided for a distinction of personal pronouns. The sentences in question are clearly defective; but they could be amended only by an excessive verbosity and tautology, which would be much more objectionable;

and, at any rate, *they are no justification of those errors of composition which might easily be amended, and which spring from the writer's own indolence or carelessness.* The confusion of personal pronouns, however, is a subject worthy of comment. It is incidentally alluded to by a writer in the last number of '*The Quarterly 'Review*', in an article on the report of the Public School Commissioners; and a ludicrous example is given, from the evidence of a Somersetshire witness in a case of manslaughter, though, notwithstanding the jumble, the sense is clear enough. The fatal affray was thus described by the peasant:—" He'd a stick, and he'd a " stick, and he licked he, and he licked he; and if he'd " a licked he as hard as he licked he, he'd a killed he, and " not he he." Now, supposing the witness not to know either combatant, one does not see how he could have expressed himself more clearly, and he would have a right to charge the defect on the language. Like everything else in the world, human speech is very imperfect, and we must sometimes take it with all its blemishes, because we can do no better. For instance, there is a certain form of expression which involves a downright impossibility, but which nevertheless is universally accepted. We cannot explain what we mean more pertinently than by referring to the phrase commonly seen painted on dead walls and palings:—" Stick no bills." Here what is intended is a prohibition; but it really takes the form of an injunction, and of an injunction to do an impossibility. We are not told to *refrain* from sticking something, or anything—we are *commanded* to stick something, and the something we are to stick is " no bills "! We are to stick on the wall or the paling something which has no existence. Let us try to imagine the process. We must first take up the nonentity in one hand, and with the other apply paste to its non-existent back; we are then to hoist it on a pole, and flatten it against a wall. Of course, the only correct expression would be, "Do not stick bills"; yet no one would seriously recommend the change. (The reader will observe that we have here unconsciously fallen into the same mode of speech. "*No one* would recommend"!) The received expression is more succinct, and it has now the sanction of time. In like manner we say, "He was "so vexed that he ate *no* dinner", and a hundred other phrases of the same character. But they are radically bad, and go far to excuse the uneducated for so frequently using the double negative. The unlettered man knows that he wants to state the negation of something, and not the affirmation, and he obscurely perceives that a species of affirmation of the very thing he wants to deny is put into his mouth by such a sentence as, "He *ate* no dinner"; so he whips in another negative, and really makes the phrase more intelligible to himself, and to those of his own class who hear him.

Let us conclude with a hope that Dean Alford and Mr. Moon have by this time made up their quarrel, and that henceforth they will unite their forces for the defence of '*The Queen's English*'.

A PLEA FOR THE QUEEN'S ENGLISH.

A Criticism from The North American Quarterly Review.

It may seem late to undertake the criticism of a book the second edition of which has been already some time before the public. But the first edition, which appeared a few years since (in 1863), although not passing without some slight notice in our literary journals, attained no American circulation, and made no impression upon our community. The enterprise of the publisher has succeeded in procuring for the work in its new form so wide a currency among us, and in attracting to it so much attention, that it becomes worth while seriously to inquire into its merits, and to estimate its right to be accepted as an authority; and this, as much for the sake of challenging a popularity and consideration which may turn out to be undeserved, as from regard to the good or the harm which the book is likely to do; for it makes no great pretensions to a wide scope, or to philosophic method and profundity. It styles itself "*Stray Notes on "Speaking and Spelling*," and is composed of desultory and loosely connected remarks on errors and controverted points in orthography, orthoëpy, and grammar, and was written in part, as its author takes pains to inform us, at chance moments of leisure, in cars and eating-houses and other such places. Criticism, it is plain, should not be disarmed by such acknowledgments, since no man, who cannot make his odd thoughts fully worth our acceptance, has a right to thrust them before us. The '*Stray Notes*' grew by degrees into their present form. They were put together first into lectures, and then became a series of articles in a monthly magazine. These attracted much notice, and called out abundant correspondence and comment, so that the successive papers took on a shape in part controversial and replicatory. The same was their fate after their collection into a volume; and the second edition is not a little altered from the first, under the process of criticism and reply. They have had, it will be seen, a rather peculiar history, calculated to provoke our curiosity.

The author is an English divine, of considerable note as critical editor and commentator of the Greek text of the New Testament, and has also acquired some fame in his earlier years as a writer of verses. We *should* naturally, then, explain to ourselves the popularity which the work has won, by the critical and scholarly ability and the elegant style it is found to display. Such qualities, added to the general and attractive interest of the subjects, ought to be enough to insure a notable career to even a heavier volume. It is unfortunate, however, for the American student, who is desirous to draw from this source valuable instruction as to the best usage of his mother-tongue, that he finds himself repelled, almost at the start, by a violent ebullition of spite against his native country. The reverend author, namely, is engaged in magnifying his office as polisher of the habits of speech of English speakers, by showing the exceeding and deep-reaching importance of attention to niceties of diction; and he holds up Americans to reprobation for "the "character and history of the nation, its blunted sense "of moral obligation and duty to man, its open disregard "of conventional right where aggrandizement is to be "obtained, and, I may now say, its reckless and fruitless "maintenance of the most cruel and unprincipled war in "the history of the world." (p. 6.) This, it is true, was written before Lee's surrender. Since the end of 1864 we have changed all that; and, in our zeal after self-improvement, we can well afford to pardon a few hard words to a "dignitary of the Church of England," who has given his ardent sympathies to the cause of Secession and Slavery, provided only he shall make good his claim to be our instructor in his proper department. Still, we cannot but form the suspicion that our author is somewhat under the dominion of class and national prejudices, and either careless of seeking information as to subjects upon which he is very ready to offer his opinion, or not acute in judging and profiting by information obtained. And further, it cannot but seriously shake our confidence in his philological acumen to find that our dreadful example is intended to "serve to show" the horrified British nation "that language is no trifle"! Our astonished inquiries into the connection of such a warning with such a lesson bring us to see that the Dean attributes our viciousness to the infelicities of our speech, since "every "important feature in a people's language is reflected in "its character and history." We had always thought, it must be owned, that the "reflection" was in the opposite direction: that character and history determined language. It is perhaps allowable to say, by a kind of figure, that a man's image in the glass is reflected in his person; and it is certain that, if we can make the image transcendently lovely, the man himself will be sure to turn out a beauty; only we cannot well reach the image save through the man himself. In like manner, if we can train the masses of a people to speak elegantly, doubtless we shall change their character vastly for the better; but the improvement will be only in a very subordinate degree due to the reflex action of language: it will rather be the direct effect of the process of education.

Our suspicions of the soundness of our philological authority, thus aroused, are not precisely lulled to sleep by an examination of the other incentives he offers to exactness of speech. We are pointed to the example of the Apostle Peter, when accused by the bystanders of being a Galilean, on the ground of his Galilean dialect. "So that," says our author "the fact of a provincial "pronunciation was made use of to bring about the "repentance of an erring Apostle." It is not easy to see the point of the argument here made. One might rather be tempted to infer that a provincial pronunciation is a good thing, and deserves encouragement, if it could become the means of so important a conversion; who knows but that our own local idioms, carefully nursed and duly displayed, may somehow be made to work out our salvation? But there is a worse difficulty behind; and really, if Mr. Alford were not a Dean and an editor of the New Testament text, we should be inclined to accuse him of neglecting his Bible. According to the received reading of the Evangelists, (we have not examined Dean Alford's edition,) the charge brought against the saint that he did not talk good Jerusalem Hebrew, had for its sole effect to draw from him a repetition of his former lying denial along with a volley of oaths and curses (luckless Peter! he forgot that his native dialect would only show more distinctly in such an outbreak of passion); and it was the crowing of the cock that brought about his repentance. So that, after all, the lesson we learn must be that, if we will only repress our local peculiarities of speech, we shall be less exposed to being detected in our wickedness; or else, that we must beware of accusing any one of dialectic inaccuracies, lest thereby we drive him to greater enormity of sin. Our author has perverted, without appreciable gain, a text which would not bend to his purpose in its true form.

We are now tempted to examine the other case in this department, cited by the Dean, and see whether it will not, perhaps, give us a higher idea of his qualifications as a critic of language. He speaks (p. 7 seq.) of the spurious poems of Rowley as having been in part detected by their containing the word *its*,—a word which was not in good use in Rowley's time. So far, all is well. But then he goes on to discourse concerning the infrequency of *its* in early English, and the employment of *his* for it, evidently in total ignorance of the reason, namely, that *his* was in Anglo-Saxon, and hence also for a long time in English, the regular genitive case of *it* (A. S. *hit*), not less than of *he;* and that the introduction of *its* was a popular inaccuracy, a grammatical blunder, such as the introduction of *she's* for *her* would be now. To the general apprehension, *his* stood in the usual relation of a possessive case, formed by an added *'s* to *he*, and had nothing to do with *it;* and so, popular use manufactured a new regular possessive for *it*, which was finally, after a protracted struggle, received into cultivated and literary styles, and made good English. Hear, on the other hand, our author's explanation of the rarity of *its* during the period from Shakespeare to Milton: "The reason, I suppose, "being, that possession, indicated by the possessive case "*its*, seemed to imply a certain life or personality, which "things neuter could hardly be thought of as having." A more fantastic and baseless suggestion is rarely made; it is so empty of meaning that we can hardly forbear to call it silly. There was not at that period a neuter noun in the language that did not form a possessive in *'s* with perfect freedom. Who can fancy Shakespeare doubting whether a table, as well as a horse or a man, really had or possessed legs; or as being willing to say "a table's 'legs," but questioning the propriety of "a table on *its* 'legs"? or how were the Bible translators avoiding the ascription of possession to things inanimate by talking of "the candlestick, *his* shaft and *his* branch," and so forth, instead of "*its* shaft and *its* branch"?

APPENDIX. 181

If these, then, are fair specimens of our author's learning and method, we must expect to find his book characterized by ignorance of the history of English speech, inaccuracy, loose and unsound reasoning, and weakness of linguistic insight. And we are constrained to acknowledge that such expectations will be abundantly realized in the course of a further perusal of the work. Let us cite a few more specimens.

Perhaps the most striking example we can select of the Dean's want of knowledge on philological subjects is his treatment of the word *neighbor*. "This," he says (p. 12), "has come from the German *nachbar!*" but he adds in a foot-note that the derivation has been questioned; that a Danish correspondent thinks it should be referred to the Danish or Norse *nabo;* and he has himself chanced to observe "that the dictionaries derive it from the "Anglo-Saxon *nehyebur*." He does not venture to judge of a matter of such intricacy, and simply leaves in the text his original etymology from the German. This is very much as if we were to be in doubt whether to trace a friend's descent from his grandfather, or from one or other of his second-cousins, finally inclining to a certain cousin, because with him we ourselves happened to be also somewhat acquainted. Certainly one who can display such ignorance of the first principles of English etymology ought to be condemned to hold his peace for ever on all questions concerning the English language.

The case is the same wherever a knowledge of the history of English words ought to be made of avail in discussing and deciding points of varying usage. Thus, when inquiring (p. 46 seq.) whether we ought to say *a historian* or *an historian*, and instancing the Bible use of *an* before initial *h* in almost all cases, he omits to point out that *an* is the original form; once used before both consonants and vowels, and that, when it came by degrees to be dropped before consonants, for the sake of a more rapid and easy utterance, it maintained itself longest before the somewhat equivocal aspiration, *h*. He is right, we think, in not regarding the rule for using *an* before the initial *h* of an unaccented syllable as a peremptory one. The better reason is on the side of the more popular colloquial usage; if the *h* of *historian*, like that of *history*, is to be really pronounced, made audible, *a* ought properly to stand before it, as before the other. But no Biblical support can make of such a combination as *an hero* aught but the indefensible revival of an antique and discarded way of speaking.

So, also, Dean Alford (p. 48) fails to see and to point out that, in the antiquated phrase *such an one*, we have a legacy from the time when *one* had not yet acquired its anomalous pronunciation *wŭn*, but was sounded *ōne* (as it still is in its compounds *ōnly, alōne, atōne*, etc.) As we now utter the word, *such an one* is not less absurd and worthy of summary rejection from usage than would be *such an wonder*.

The discussion, again, of "better than *I*" or "better "than *me*" is carried on (p. 152 seq.) without an allusion to the fact that *than* is historically an adverb only, the same word with *then*, and has no hereditary right to govern an accusative, as if it were a preposition. "He is "better *than* I" is, by origin, "he is better, *then* I,"—that is to say, "I next after him." Linguistic usage has, indeed, a perfect right to turn the adverbial construction into a prepositional; but, as the former is still in almost every case not only admissible, but more usual, the tendency to convert the word into a preposition is not one to be encouraged, but rather, and decidedly, the contrary.

It might be deemed unfair to blame our author for his equally faulty discussion of the question between the two forms of locution, "it is *I*" and "it is *me*," because his correspondents and the correspondents of some of the English literary journals (which have been the arena of a controversy upon the subject much more ardent than able, within no long time past) are just as far as he is from doing themselves credit in connection with it. What he cites from Latham, and (in a note) from Ellis, is tolerably pure twaddle. It may well enough be that "it is *me*" is now already so firmly established in colloquial usage, and even in written, that the attempt to oust it will be in vain; but the expression is none the less in its origin a simple blunder, a popular inaccuracy. It is neither to be justified nor palliated by theoretical considerations,—as by alleging a special predicative construction, or by citing French and Danish parallels. There was a time when to say "*us* did it" for "*we* did it," "*them* did it" for "*they* did it," was just as correct as to say "*you* did it" for "*ye* did it"; but usage, to which we must all bow as the only and indisputable authority in language, has ratified the last corruption and made it good English, while rejecting the other two. He would be a pedant who should insist in these days that we ought to say *ye* instead of *you* in the nominative; but he would also have been worthy of ridicule who, while the change was in progress, should have supported it on the ground of a tendency to the subjective use of the accusative, and cited in its favor the example of the Italian *loro*, "them," for *elleno*, "they," as plural of respectful address. And as long as it is still vulgar to say "it is "*him*," "it is *her*," "it is *us*," "it is *them*," and still proper and usual to say "it is *I*," our duty as favorers of good English requires us to oppose and discountenance "it is *me*," with the rest of its tribe, as all alike regretable and avoidable solecisms.

Of course the Dean puts his veto (p. 253) upon *reliable;* men of his stamp always do. He alleges the staple argument of his class, that *rely-upon-able* would be the only legitimate form of such a derivative from *rely*. They ought fairly to put the case somewhat thus: "It is *un-account-for-able*, not to say *laugh-at-able*, that men will try to force upon the language a word so *take-objection-to-able*, so little *avail-of-able*, and so far from *indispense-with-able*, as *reliable*"; then we should see more clearly how much the plea is worth.

Of course, again, our author sets his face like flint against writing *or* instead of *our* at the end of such words as *honor* and *favor;* and that upon the high and commanding consideration that to simplify the termination thus "is part of a movement to reduce our spelling to "uniform rule as opposed to usage" (p. 10); that it "is "an approach to that wretched attempt to destroy all "the historic interest of our language, which is known "by the name of *phonetic* spelling" (p. 14),—and upon the phonetic movement he proceeds to pour out the vials of his ponderous wit and feeble denunciation. On the whole, we think the phonetists are to be congratulated on having the Dean for an adversary; his hostility is more a credit to them than would be his support. There are a host of difficulties in the way of the phonetic spellers which they themselves, or many of them, are far from appreciating; but they are not of the kind which Mr. Alford seeks to raise. No one wants to set up rule against usage, but only to change usage from a bad rule to a good one. And our language has a store of historic interest which would not be perceptibly trenched upon, even if we were to take the liberty of writing our words just as we speak them. Our present spelling is of the nature of a great and long-established institution, so intimately bound up with the habits and associations of the community that it is well-nigh, or quite, impregnable. But a philologist ought to be ashamed to defend it on principle, on theoretical grounds. He, at any rate, ought to know that a mode of writing is no proper repository for interesting historical reminiscences; that an alphabetic system has for its office simply and solely to represent faithfully a spoken language, and is perfect in proportion as it fulfils that office, without attempting to do also the duty of Egyptian hieroglyphs and Chinese ideographs. No other so great linguistic blessing could be conferred upon the English language and the people who speak it as a consistent phonetic orthography.

It is calculated profoundly to stagger our faith in Dean Alford's capacity as an interpreter and expositor of difficult texts to find him guilty of explaining (p. 105) the reflexive verb *to endeavor one's self* by "to consider "one's self in duty bound," and of asserting that this "appears clearly" from the answer made by the candidate for ordination to the bishop's exhortation to diligence in prayer and other holy exercises, "I will *endeavor my-* "*self* so to do, the Lord being my helper." Not only does this answer exact no such interpretation of the phrase as the one given by the Dean, but it even directly and obviously suggests the true meaning, "to exert one's "self, to do one's endeavor."

A similar paucity of insight is exhibited in our author's

theory (p. 86), that the origin of the double comparative *lesser*, for *less*, is to be traced to the "attraction" of the dissyllabic word *greater*, with which it is not infrequently found connected in use. No such effect of attraction as this, we are sure, can be found in any part of our English speech. The true reason of the form is not hard to discover: it lies in the extension of a prevailing analogy to one or two exceptional cases. *Less* and *worse* are the only comparatives in our language which do not end in *r;* and *er* is accordingly so distinctly present to the apprehension of the language-users as a sign of comparative meaning that they have gone on, naturally enough, to apply it to those two also, thus assimilating them to the rest of their class. The only difference in the result is, that *lesser* has been fully adopted, in certain connections, into good usage, while *worser* is still a vulgarism.

Nor can we ascribe any greater merit to the Dean's treatment of the preposition *on to*, or *onto*, used to denote motion, as distinguished from locality or place, denoted by the simple preposition *on:* thus, "The cat "jumped *on to* the table, and danced about *on* the table." Such a distinction, as every one knows, is often made in colloquial style, but is not yet, and perhaps may never be, admitted in good writing; this tolerates only *on*. Our author is not content with denying that *on to* is now good writable English; he tries to make out there is no reason or propriety in attempting to express any such difference of relation as is signified by the two separate forms. His argument is this: if we say, "The cat jumped *on* the table," or if the tired school-boy, begging a lift on his way, gets from the coachman the permission, "All "right, jump *on* the box," will there be any danger of a failure to understand what is meant? Of course not, we reply; but neither should we fail to understand, "The "dog jumped *in* the water, and brought out the stick"; nor would Tom be slow in taking, and acting on, coachee's meaning, if the reply were, "Jump *in* the carriage." The question is not one of mere intelligibility, but of the desirableness of giving formal expression to a real difference of relation,—as we have actually done in the case of *in* and *into*. *On to,* says our author (p. 181), is not so good English as *into*, "because *on* is ordinarily a pre- "position of motion as well as of rest, whereas *in* is "almost entirely a preposition of rest." This is an amusing inversion of the real relations of the case: in fact, *in* is a preposition of rest only, because we have *into* in good usage as the corresponding preposition of motion; *on* is obliged to be both, because *onto* has not won its way to general acceptance. The double form would be just as proper and just as expressive in the one case as in the other, and there is no good reason why we should not heartily wish that *onto* were as unexceptionable English as is *into*, whether we believe or not that it will ever become so, and whether or not we are disposed to take the responsibility of joining to make it so. Every German scholar knows how nice and full of meaning are the distinctions made in the German language, as regards these two and a few other prepositions, by the use after them of a dative to denote locality, and an accusative to denote motion. The Anglo-Saxon was able to accomplish the same object by the same means; but we have, in losing our dative case, lost the power to do so, and have only partially made up the loss, by coining, during the modern period, such secondary words as *into* and *onto*, that they may bear a part of the office of *in* and *on*.

We will barely allude to one or two more instances of a like character: such as our author's conjecture (p. 67) that our separation of *mănifold* in pronunciation from *many* is due to the influence of its felt analogy with *mănifest;* his attempt (p. 91) to find an etymological reason for the translation, "Our Father *which* art in "heaven," instead of "*who* art"; his theory (p. 42) that the conjunction of the two words "humble and hearty" in the Prayer-Book is good ground for holding that the first as well as the second was pronounced with an aspirated *h;* his apparent assumption (p. 25) that the *'s* of *senator's* represent the Latin *is* of *senatoris* (or is it only his confused expression that is to blame here?),— and so forth.

These are but the more prominent and striking illustrations of Dean Alford's general method. We may say without exaggeration that—especially in the first half of the book, where questions are more often dealt with that include historical considerations and call for some scholarship—there is hardly a single topic brought under discussion which is treated in a thorough and satisfactory manner, in creditable style and spirit: even where we are agreed with respect to our author's conclusions, he repels us by a superficial, or an incomplete, or a prejudiced, or a blundering statement of the reasons that should guide us to them. It is almost an impertinence in one so little versed in English studies to attempt to teach his countrymen how they ought to speak.

The last half of the work deals prevailingly with syntactical points, requiring to be argued rather upon rhetorical than grammatical grounds. But, though in a measure exempt from the class of criticisms which we have found occasion to make above, it is not without its own faults. The dean's chief hobby throughout is the depreciation of "laws," whether of the rhetorician or of the grammarian, and the exaltation of "usage" as opposed to them. He has, of course, a certain right on his side, yet not precisely as he understands it. The laws he rejects are only meant to stand as expressions of good usage; nor do those who set them up arrogate to them peremptory and universal force, but rather a value as guiding principles, attention to which will save, from many faults, the less wary and skilful. No one holds that he who has not native capacity and educated taste can become by their aid an elegant writer; no one denies that he who has capacity and taste may cast them to the winds, sure that his own sense of what is right will lead him to clear and forcible expression. But we have all heard of a class of people who inveigh against "laws," and would fain escape judgment by them; and the very vigor of the Dean's recalcitrations inspires us with suspicions that there may be good cause for his uneasiness. And so it is: he has not in any eminent degree that fine sense which enables one to write without rule a pure and flowing English. His style is always heavy and ungraceful, and often marked with infelicities and even with inaccuracies. As many of our readers are aware, he has received on this score a terrible scathing from Mr. Moon, in a little work happily entitled "*The Dean's English,*" by way of answer to "*The Queen's English.*" To this we refer any one who may be curious to see, properly exposed, the other side of the Dean's claim to set himself up as a critic of good English. The professed general views he puts forth are in no small part special pleadings, rather, against the criticisms of his censors. He appears to suppose that any somewhat inaccurate or slovenly phrase or construction of his for which he can find parallels in our Bible translation and in Shakespeare is thereby hallowed and made secure against attack, unmindful that our style of expression has in many points tended towards precision and nicety during the last centuries, so that not everything which was allowed in Shakespeare's time will be tolerated now.

It is our opinion, therefore, upon the whole, that the English-speaking public would have lost little had our author's lucubrations been confined to the "Church of England Young Men's Literary Association," for which they were originally intended, and which doubtless received them with unquestioning faith. The circulation and credit they have won in this country are mainly a reflection of the unusual attention which has been paid them in England; and the latter is partly fortuitous, the result of a combination of favoring circumstances, partly due to the general interest felt in the subject of the work, and a curiosity to hear what a man of high position and repute for scholarship has to say upon it; and in part it is an indication of the general low state of philological culture in the British Isles. We cannot wish "*The Queen's English*" a continued currency, unless it be understood and received by all for just what it is,—a simple expression of the views and prejudices of a single educated Englishman respecting matters of language; having, doubtless, a certain interest and value as such, but possessing no more authority than would belong to a like expression on the part of any one among thousands of its readers. Its true character is that of *a sample of private opinion, and not a guide and model of general usage.*

THE QUEEN'S ENGLISH AND THE DEAN'S ENGLISH.

A Criticism from 'The Biblical Repertory,' Philadelphia, U. S. A.

'*A Plea for the Queen's English,*' or '*Stray Notes on Speaking and Spelling,*' is a collection of papers originally delivered as lectures to the Church of England Young Men's Literary Association at Canterbury, by Dr. Alford, Dean of Canterbury. They were afterwards published in '*Good Words,*' and now appear in a volume under the above title, but considerably modified in form. '*The Dean's English*' consists of a series of criticisms upon the Dean's Essays as they appeared in '*Good Words.*' They were written by Mr. G. Washington Moon, F.R.S.L., who considered it his duty to expose the errors of the Dean, lest others should be injured by the example of "one of exalted position and reputed "learning." The sharp controversy that ensued attracted public attention throughout the English literary world, and the discussion has been of much service. The verdict of the literary public in England, upon nearly all the points in controversy, has been in favour of the critic and against the Dean.

We read the Dean's work very carefully, and made our own criticisms as we read. Upon taking up Mr. Moon's little work we, of course, found we had been anticipated in most of them, and were pleased to have the weight of his authority to sustain our judgment. There are, doubtless, many excellent things in '*The Queen's English,*' to which we should do well to take heed; the style of the author, however, is not only inelegant, but even inaccurate and slovenly. We are surprised that the Dean's work should be employed as a text-book in some of our institutions of learning. It contains scores of errors, and surely the text-book should not only inculcate correct principles, but be an exemplification of them. If the Dean's book be employed for purposes of instruction, the critic's work, which is almost faultless in point of style, and rarely incorrect in its views, ought by all means to accompany it; bane and antidote should go together. In a subsequent part of this article we shall present proofs of the Dean's want of qualifications for the position he has assumed, beyond those of any person of ordinary scholarship and correct taste.

The English language is spoken by nearly sixty millions of men, and "appears destined hereafter to "prevail with a sway more extensive than even its "present, over all the portions of the globe." Jacob Grimm, the highest authority in the Gothic languages, declares that "in wealth, wisdom, and strict economy, "none of the living languages can vie with it." Its simple syntax, the small number of its grammatical forms, its nervous power, and its massive strength, point it out as a "world-language," which has already fulfilled the prophecy of its earlier days:—

> "Who knows whither we may vent
> "The treasure of our tongue? To what strange shores
> "This gain of our best glory may be sent
> "T' enrich unknowing nations with our stores?
> "What worlds in the yet unformed Occident
> "May come refined with accents that are ours?" *

A language of such richness and power, the vehicle of more free thought and earnest truth than any other

* Daniel, in De Vere's 'Studies in English,' page 1.

living language, is worthy of our most diligent study. And yet it is only within a few years that the attention of scholars has been directed to the thorough investigation upon philosophical principles of that language, which, within four centuries from the time it ceased to be a mere jargon, produced the greatest poet of modern times.

Everyone who has had even a superficial acquaintance with our schools and colleges, knows that scarcely any branch of education is more neglected than the study of our vernacular tongue. Young men can neither spell correctly nor write grammatically, and the deficiency is as great, and the evil is as crying, in this department as in the classical instruction of many of our schools and academies. It is taken for granted that men will know how to spell and to write their own language without any instruction. Not in America only is this the case, but in England also, where there are loud complaints about the neglect of the study of their own language and literature. Not only are degrees conferred upon men who cannot translate their diplomas; but Senior Wranglers, First Class men, and others, go forth from the universities with the ability to write faultless Latin prose or perfect Greek iambics, while they are unable to write even a letter in grammatical English. More attention is paid to the subject of English composition in the colleges of this country than in those of England, but it is impossible for them to remedy the deficiencies of the earlier stages of education. The thorough study of the classical languages need not interfere with attention to our own in the academy; and every college should have a Chair of the English Language and Literature.

Despite all the causes of alienations, both in the

earlier and in the later history of England and America, the bonds of union between the two countries are growing stronger. The ocean between them does not divide, but unites them more closely. They are Anglo-Saxon in their national traits, and their unity is manifest in the essential oneness of the language that exhibits the characteristics of their nationality. This language is a common inheritance, and the nations that speak it have a right to add to its stores. When a language ceases to grow, it begins to decay. The English language has not yet reached this stage of its development, and as long as there is vitality in the American people they will contribute to its growth; and much of what originates here, must be accepted upon the other side of the ocean as a legitimate outgrowth from the common stock. Even our English critics are beginning to confess the right of America to make contributions to the language, and to acknowledge the lawful claims of these new words and phrases, to a position in the tongue which is not the exclusive heritage of Englishmen. Considering the nature of language, the character of our people, and the constant infusion of "strange tongues," it is surprising that the language has not suffered greater changes at our hands than it exhibits at present. Englishmen exaggerate the changes, while many Americans either deny them or attempt to explain them, and retort by directing attention to the numerous errors in language prevalent in England. Dean Alford's book certainly shows that not a few solecisms, and these by no means trivial, are to be met with even amongst educated persons in England. The English language as spoken in America, undoubtedly has some peculiarities; but to collect all the expressions to be found in American books or newspapers, or to be heard in the colloquial language of this country, that differs from the language of the best English authors, and to call these Americanisms, and to denounce us as corrupters of the English tongue, is manifestly unjust. The colloquial language of the two countries differs much more than the written language. We have common standards for the one, while in the other, the racy, idiomatic expressions have been lost by reason of our separation, and their places have frequently been supplied by the strong but inelegant expressions that may, too often, be designated as slang. Bartlett has gathered from all sources, but chiefly from the humorous writers of this country, many hundreds of words and phrases, which he styles Americanisms. Many of them, however, are really good English; and surely the slang expressions of this country no more represent the language of America, than does the *argot* of some of the low characters of Eugene Sue's novels represent the language of the cultivated class of the French capital, or the "flash" language of London low life represent that of elegant society in the West End. Slang and even archaic modes of expression ought to be excluded from any just estimate of the "deterioration "which the Queen's English has undergone at the hands "of the Americans." And yet these, we think, constitute the great body of the corruptions which we are charged with having introduced.

It is undoubtedly true that the English language is spoken much more correctly by the mass of the people in America than by the corresponding class in England; but it is also true that the best educated people in England deviate less frequently from the standard of good English than do our best scholars in America. In other words, the educated class employ better English in their conversation, not in their writings, than the same class in America. Although dialects do not exist among us, and the language has achieved a remarkable degree of purity and uniformity, yet there are peculiarities that distinguish the different sections of the country. The nasal intonation of New England, the omission of the *h* after *w* in the Middle States, the drawl of the Southern, and the peculiar accent of the Western States, seem to us to mark unmistakably the inhabitants of the different parts of the land.

While noticing the errors either of Dean Alford himself, or those to which he calls attention, it may be well to glance at some of the mistakes that are made even by well-educated people among ourselves. The Dean, in ungrammatical English, condemns the practice of omitting the "*u*" in the termination "*our.*" He hopes, with Archdeacon Hare, that the "abomination will be confined "to the cards of the great vulgar, and to books printed "in America."

Recent investigation, however, shows that spelling *honor, favor,* &c., without the "*u*" is not an Americanism, for it actually prevailed in the sixteenth and seventeenth centuries. Although sympathizing with the Dean in his view, we think it useless to attempt to stem the current. One word, we trust, will be kept sacred from this innovation. An Englishman once remarked, "We scarcely "know our *Saviour* in your American language." "By "removing a single letter from the holy word Saviour, "you would shock the piety of millions," says Johnson in Landor. Let the word "*Saviour*" at least remain intact; we will yield the others without discussing the question of their derivation from Latin or French originals.

The next subject which the Dean takes up is that of pronunciation. Anyone who has met Englishmen even casually, has been struck with the difference between their mode of pronunciation and that of Americans. The English *clip* their words, the Americans enunciate every syllable distinctly; the English articulate the consonants plainly; the Americans dwell upon the vowels. It is certain that we are more easily understood by foreigners, and that we acquire the pronunciation of foreign languages with greater facility. The French say that the English can rarely enunciate the French sounds correctly, while the Americans are next to the Russians and the Poles in the ease with which they acquire a command of the language. Whether this is merely the language of compliment or not, we are unable to say. Whatever may be our faults in pronunciation, we are free from that which the Dean pronounces the worst of all, the misuse of the aspirate, the exasperating "exhas-"piration," as it has been termed. It is remarkable that the English are not the only people who have engaged in this war of extermination. Among the ancient Greeks and Romans the tendency of the vulgar was to omit the aspirate in the words to which it belongs, and the sound of "h" is no longer heard in the languages of Southern Europe. The best authorities deny this letter any power in French, save that of preventing the elision of the vowel of the article, or the *liaison*, in connection with the words beginning with the so-called aspirate "h." England then does not stand alone in this respect, and the history of the language proves that the error existed several centuries since.

Although we do not have the same trouble as the English in reference to the "h," yet in the Middle

States the words beginning with "*wh*" are very generally pronounced incorrectly. The same error prevails in England, although not to so great an extent. Thus, no distinction is made between *when* and *wen*, *whet* and *wet*, *white* and *wight*, *wheel* and *weal*, *which* and *witch*, *whine* and *wine;* although the words contrast ludicrously enough when pronounced together. By recalling the fact that originally the "*h*" preceded the "*w*" in the orthography, as it still does in the correct pronunciation, the difficulty will be obviated. We are not noticing the faults of the vulgar and ignorant, so much as those of educated persons. In the English House of Parliament, and in good society in this country, one may hear such expressions as the "*lawr* of the land," the "*idear* of a "God," "*Jehovahr*," "*peninsular*," &c., as if persons were unwilling, or did not have sufficient energy, to cut off the sound when they arrive at the end of a word. In the Southern States, on the contrary, the tendency is to omit the "*r*" at the end of words, *e.g.*, *doah* instead of *door*, although we believe that even in New York the final "*r*" is often transformed into "*h*."

We may here notice a group of errors in reference to the sound of "*o*"; these are *doos* for *does*, chiefly in Connecticut; *nŏthing* for *nothing (nŭthing,)* throughout New England; *Lard* for *Lord* also in New England; *hoarse* and *moarning* for *horse* and *morning*, both in New Jersey; *pore* for *poor*, in the South. These may seem small things, and yet they indicate the finished and accurate scholar. The English pronounce the name of God very short, *Gŏd*, while the Americans prolong the "*o*" and pronounce the word as if written *Gawd*. The English may be correct, but it is too late for us to rectify the error, if it is one.

APPENDIX. 199

In France there is an Academy to preserve the language in its purity and propriety; in Germany the stage regulates the language to a considerable extent; while in England the usage of the learned professions and of Parliament is the ordinary standard of appeal. But in this country, at least outside of our great cities, the ministry exerts more influence upon the pronunciation of the language than any other class of society. It is of the utmost importance, then, that they should be "ensamples to the flock" in language, as well as in conduct; and while seeking to amend the life, they should not corrupt the speech of the people. Ministers often pronounce incorrectly the proper names of Scripture. We coincide with the Dean in considering this fault as inexcusable, because a reference to the original at once decides the pronunciation. It would, however, be pure affectation to pronounce Alexandrĭa, Philadelphĭa, Samarĭa, &c., because English usage differs from the original in the pronunciation of these names. It is unpardonable in a minister to murder the name of *Daniel* by pronouncing it in two syllables. It is certainly great cruelty *to knock out* its "*i*", especially as it is a *Cyclops*. *Pharaoh*, on the contrary, is a dissyllable. Some persons, through a desire to avoid what they conceive to be a vulgarism, pronounce the "*t*" in "*apostle*," "*epistle*," and "*often.*" It is, however silent, and this "licensed "barbarism" is the only correct mode of pronouncing these words. The words "covetous" and "covetous-"ness" are often mangled by inserting an "*i*" in pronouncing them "*covetious*" and "*covetiousness*", and to these we may add "*heinious*" and "*heiniousness.*"

We may mention here, incidentally, that in the attempt to correct this awful pronunciation, the Dean's original paragraph was so ambiguously worded, that Mr. Moon demonstrated mathematically that it was susceptible of 10,240 different readings. The Dean had the good sense to amend his sentence in the second edition, and we sincerely wish that he had more frequently heeded the advice of his critic.

The next topic discussed in his work is that of idioms. He defines an idiom to be " some saying, or some way of "speaking, peculiar to some one language or family of "languages, which can only be accounted for by the peculiar "tendency, or habit of thought, of those who use it." We are careful in giving his definition, because the term is employed in a different sense. It is used strictly to denote the sum of the rules of construction, or that general syntax of the language which constitutes its peculiar character, and does not simply mean those forms of expression which cannot be explained by the ordinary rules, either of general grammar or by those of the particular language in which the phrases occur.

Accepting, however, the Dean's definition of the term, we do not see how he can argue from an idiom in one language to that in another, or prove that because an idiom is common in one language that it ought to prevail, or at least is not incorrect, in another. Because attraction, direct or inverse, is constantly occurring in Greek, and gives unity to the sentence and beauty to the language, that is not a valid reason for its introduction into English. It is a peculiarity, an *idiom* of the Greek tongue. In reference to the neuter plural* with the singular verb in Greek, to which he alludes, we may

---

* In certain instances when the subject was not neuter the verb might be singular, provided it preceded its subject, as in the French idom, *Il y a des hommes.*

remark that the rule was not absolute; when the individuals composing the mass were considered as *one body*, the verb was in the singular number, but when they were viewed otherwise, or possessed life, it was put in the plural. On the contrary, when an infinitive or a part of a sentence is the subject, the predicate adjective is usually in the plural, although the copula is singular. His mode of argument then seems to us to have but little weight in the cases in which he employs it. You may argue from the *general laws* of language, but certainly not from the *idioms* of one language to those of another, except of course in the case of dialects, or even languages having a common and a not very remote origin. This principle, which we think correct, is a sufficient and complete answer to his plea in favour of "*these kind,*" and "*those kind,*" expressions which even the Dean, and those who side with him in his views, would not employ in a polite circle or before a cultivated audience.

To notice all the matters which the Dean brings up, would extend this article beyond due proportions. There is a point in reference to the so-called double comparative "*lesser*," in respect to which we think he is in error. He regards its use as "an idiomatic irregularity which "we must be content to tolerate." We think that "*lesser*" is the original, and "*less*" is the intruder. Our translators did not merely "sanction the usage," but were perfectly correct when they wrote, "God made "two great lights: the greater light to rule the day, and "the *lesser* light to rule the night;" for both *less* and *least* are contractions of *leaser* (or *lesser*), and *leasest,* regular forms from the now obsolete *leas* or *less*, and the fuller form was the one employed by the best writers of that day. In fact the form *lesser* is always employed in the Bible when it qualifies a noun *following;* and Shakespeare, we believe, uses it oftener than he does the form *less.* The grammarians whom the Dean takes every occasion to denounce, and for whose rules he expresses supreme contempt, do not stand in need of his commiseration so much as he imagines. Had he observed their precepts more generally he would not have been guilty of so many errors, and thus have rendered himself liable to so much just criticism. The strict grammarian, who has studied his vernacular language, does not find it so difficult to give a satisfactory explanation of the "idiomatic expression" "*methinks,*" as the Dean would lead us to believe. The impersonal use of the verb, which he considers so strange, was quite common in the Anglo-Saxon, although it now exists in English only in *methinks, meseems,* and *melists.* It was, doubtless, an imitation, or rather a relic, of the Latin. The Dean may be surprised to learn that *methinks,* in the opinion of some of the best grammarians, has no connection with the verb *to think.* *To think* is the Anglo-Saxon *thencan=denken* in German, while *methinks* is derived from the Anglo-Saxon *thincan,* meaning *to seem.* *Methinks,* therefore, means *it seems to me,* the *me* corresponding to the dative in similar expressions in Latin and in Greek, *e.g., mihi videtur,* μοι δοχεῖ; and it was even correct to say, *videor mihi,* δοχῶ μοι, *i.e., methinks. Methought* arose from the mistaken notion as to the origin of *methinks.*

The contraction "*I'd*" is sometimes resolved into "*I had,*" instead of "*I would,*" which is, of course, the correct expression. Landor represents Tooke as criticising Johnson for his error upon this point. "T.

"Permit me first to ask whether we can say, I *had hear?*
"J. You mean to say *heard*. T. No: I mean the words
"I *had hear*. J. Why ask me so idle a question? T.
"Because I find in the eighth chapter of *Rasselas*, 'I
"'*had* rather *hear* thee dispute.' The intervention of
"*rather* cannot make it more or less proper. J. Sir, you
"are right."

The Dean is peculiarly unfortunate both in his quotations and in his appeals to Scripture. He declares (and in this opinion he is not alone) that the pronoun "*its*" does not occur in the Bible, and Leviticus xxv, 5, is at once cited against him; he founds an argument, in favour of his erroneous view as to the correct mode of placing an adverb, upon an alleged expression in Scripture, and when it is referred to, it is found to sustain the view of his adversary and to be diametrically opposed to his own. It is Numbers xii, 2, "And they said, Hath the Lord "indeed spoken *only* by Moses?" *Only* is correctly placed, but not so in the judgment of the Dean, who had it "only spoken." He quotes from Milton,

"Which, when Beëlzebub perceived, *than whom*,
"Satan except, none higher sat."

But it has been well remarked that he did not quote from the same author,

"What matter where, if I be still the same,
"And what I should be, all but less *than he*."

We may also furnish a quotation or two from Shakespeare:

"Am I not an inch of fortune better than she?"
"Well, if you were but an inch of fortune better than I, where
"would you choose it?"

The Dean says, "And thus everyone of us would "speak: 'than who' would be intolerable. And this "seems to settle the question." By no means. A poet, whose latest work was highly commended in our last number, and who is also the Professor of Latin at Oxford, and should by reason both of his attainments and his position be an authority in the matter of language, thus writes:

"Æneas was our king, than *who*
"The breath of being none e'er drew,
"More brave, more pious, or more true."

And again:

"The son of Æolus, than *who*
"None ere more skilled the trumpet blew
"To animate the warrior crew,
   "And martial fire relume."

Is it not probable that, as some one has suggested, "*than whom*" is only a traditional typographical error, which has become almost fixed in the language, like "*strain at*" instead of "*strain out*" a gnat in Scripture? The most amusing thing, however, in connection with this subject is, that the Dean himself fell into the correct grammatical usage upon the very first page of his book, and that he might be consistent with his own views he changed the form of expression. Originally it stood "*than you or I*," and he afterwards changed it to "*any* "*one of us*." Of course the intervention of "*or*" does not affect the principle of construction. Appeal has been made to the construction of the comparative degree with the genitive in Greek and Latin, an idiom which we translate into English by "*than*." But it is precisely in the construction in which the particle corresponding to "*than*" is *omitted* that we employ the oblique case. The particle "*as*" is used in the same manner as "*than*," and we can all recall the amusing mistakes made by our Teutonic friends who are constantly confounding these conjunctions. If the phrase "*he is better than him*" is correct, then so is the phrase "*he is as good as her;*" and the next thing we shall see or hear is some unbreeched Highlander stalking across the English border, as of old, and insisting that he is perfectly correct in saying, "*her is* "*as good as him.*"

It will not do to say that the Dean is pleading only for colloquial English, such as is heard at the fireside and in the family circle. For in paragraphs 124, 125, 126, he gives directions for punctuation, and in 380 and elsewhere he gives advice about style of writing, &c. Even were he advocating the claims of genuine colloquial English, surely that is no reason why ungrammatical or vulgar language should be suggested for our use. Of all places, (the Dean would say " of all *other* places,") the fireside is that at which we should speak correctly. In the bosom of the family let no slang expressions, no vulgar colloquialisms, no solecisms, no incorrect pronunciations, be heard by our children, or be permitted to issue from their lips without correction, and it will be as easy for them to speak with propriety as for them to act with propriety. "Train up a child in the way he "should go, and when he is old he will not depart "from it."

In connection with this point we may allude to another error in the use of the pronouns, and one which is by no means uncommon. Persons remembering the impropriety of saying, "*you and me*", when these pronouns constitute the subject of the verb, fall into the habit of placing "*you and I*" in the nominative, when they should be in the objective in the expression "*between you and me*". So also "I thought it was *him*," instead of *he;* "I took "it to be *he*", instead of *him*.

In England, professors *teach* their pupils, they do not *learn* them, although the Anglo-Saxon *læran* did originally mean *to teach*, and Shakespeare says,—

"Sweet prince, you learn me noble thankfulness."

The distinction between the verbs *to teach* and *to learn* had not been so clearly defined as is the case at present. In this passage they are precisely synonymous:—"Unless you could *teach* me to forget a banished father, you must not *learn* me how to remember any extraordinary pleasure."

In England both *donate* and "donation visits" are unknown, the verbs *loan* and *jeopardize* are not employed, but that "vile vocable *talented*," as Coleridge calls it, is stealing into good society and attempting to introduce along with itself, *gifted*, *moneyed*, &c. The English use *grow* in a transitive sense, and it is already found in our agricultural papers. Not long since we heard an Irishman speak of *labouring* the potatoes. Enough, however, upon these minor points: we add only, that "*once and again*" is correct, not "*time and again*," and that "*got*" is superfluous in the expression, "*I have "got*"=*I possess*.

The Dean very justly condemns the use of the terms "party" and "individual" for "man," and yet he is charged by Mr. Moon with being himself guilty of the offence. In "business" circles in New York the term party is constantly employed where it is not desirable to name the person alluded to. The use of the term *"female,"* to denote a woman, he very justly censures. Applied to a woman, it would be considered, in France, an insult sufficient to provoke a duel.

The *London 'Times'* is almost an authority in England in the matter of good English, but while the editorials in some of our journals are admirable in point of style, yet many of our papers do not think it necessary to be even grammatical in the expression of their views. De Quincy, in one of his articles, gives an amusing account of the language of a landlady from whom he attempted to hire lodgings. Her speech was in the highest and most ornate style of the newspapers. A consummate master of English and with a wealth of language that is truly astonishing, he could himself use long words, and he endured her talk for some time; but at length he grew nervous, and when she made use of the adverb *anteriorly* he could endure no more, and in despair rushed from the house. The same writer states what is very true, that in the nursery is to be found the most idiomatic English, and that the correspondence of educated women contains some of the best specimens of the language.* This is true, perhaps, of all cultivated languages; even the style of Cicero owed much of its excellence to his association with some of the noblest ladies of Rome, while the purity of ancient Greek lingered longest among the women and children of Constantinople.

The English Bible has exerted upon the English

* "Would you desire," he says, "at this day to read our noble lan- "guage in its native beauty, picturesque from idiomatic propriety, racy "in its phraseology, delicate yet sinewy in its composition—steal the "mail-bags, and break open all the letters in female handwriting."

language a greater influence than any other book that was ever written, and has contributed more to keep the language pure, and to prevent any divergence in speech from manifesting itself among the distant colonies of England, than all other causes combined. The Dean in his attacks upon the grammarians considers himself the special champion of the language of the Bible and of Shakespeare. He must have been unfortunate in the few grammarians whom he consulted, for we can recall but one who does not select his instances of false syntax from the Bible. We condemn the practice, but we cannot agree with the Dean, who thinks that because an expression is found in the Bible it must therefore be correct English. This reminds us of the old controversy in reference to the Greek of the New Testament. One party contended that it was as pure and correct as that of the writers of Attic Greek, because they considered it derogatory to the Holy Spirit to suppose that any grammatical or other errors could occur; while the other party contended that it was utterly corrupt, abounding in Hebraisms, &c. The truth in this case, as in most others, is between the extreme views. It is the current Greek language of the day in which it was written, coloured by the Jewish minds through which the new Christian ideas were communicated to the world by the Holy Spirit. The errors in language did not affect the truth revealed, and they were just such as men in the position of the authors would be likely to make. So with the English version of the Bible. Its translators seem to have been almost inspired, and the English Bible will ever stand as the purest and best specimen of the speech of which it is an ornament and an example. As is the Greek of the New Testament so is the English of our Bible; each is admirable for its purpose, but it is not perfect. We think that a better translation can never be made: but this is not to say that there may not be a few inaccurate renderings of the original, or a few places in which the English may not be improved. We cannot refrain from quoting the eulogy of our English Bible by one who has given up the faith and the Bible of his ancestors. "Who will not say that the uncommon "beauty and marvellous English of the Protestant Bible "is not one of the great strongholds of heresy in this "country? It lives on the ear, like a music that can "never be forgotten, like the sound of church bells, "which the convert hardly knows how he can forego. Its "felicities often seem to be almost things rather than "mere words. It is part of the national mind, and the "anchor of national seriousness. . . . . The memory of "the dead passes into it. The potent traditions of child-"hood are stereotyped in its verses. The power of all "the griefs and trials of a man is hidden beneath its "words. It is the representative of his best moments, "and all that there has been about him of soft, and gentle, "and pure, and penitent, and good, speaks to him for "ever out of his English Bible. . . . . It is his sacred "thing, which doubt has never dimmed, and controversy "never soiled. In the length and breadth of the land "there is not a Protestant with one spark of religiousness "about him, whose spiritual biography is not in his "Saxon Bible." *

But we must hasten to finish this review of the Dean's peculiar views. We are surprised that after noticing and correcting so many errors prevalent even amongst educated men, he should discourage the study of grammar

* Newman, quoted in Trench's "English Past and Present," p. 34.

and rhetoric, and refer men to "common sense, ordinary "observation, and the prevailing usage of the English "people," as good guides in the matter of writing English. In the earlier stages of education at least, men must receive most of their knowledge upon authority, and it is only after they have made considerable progress in any branch of study that they can investigate and ascertain principles for themselves. Most men, moreover, do not enjoy the peculiar social and literary advantages which in the estimation of the Dean are better than treatises on grammar and rhetoric. Even Milton is not an authority in orthography, for his delicate ear sacrificed the spelling of words to his magnificent rhythm; while Shakespeare does not hesitate to violate the ordinary rules of orthoepy for the sake of the metre. Transcendent genius like theirs may be pardoned for such faults, but inferior men must not expect forgiveness when they commit similar errors. Because Milton sang:

> Adam the goodliest man of men since born
> His sons, the fairest of her daughters Eve;

or because Thucydides calls the Peloponnesian war ἀξιολογώτατον τῶν προγεγενημένων, we are not justified in using the superlative when the comparative is the correct form. Even with the Dean in our favour we should not be justified in speaking of Thucydides as the one writer of *all. other* good Attic writers who is the most ungrammatical. Examples of similar mistakes can be found in all languages, and even in the best writers, but they are none the less mistakes. We know the meaning of the expression of Tacitus, *Ceterorum Britannorum fugacissimi*, but we should not imitate it.

The Dean and some of his friends seem to think if they can find in a good author a form of expression violating the ordinary rules of grammar, that such a phrase is correct and must straightway be admitted into "the society of good English." It seems to us that all that such a discovery proves is, that a good writer has made a mistake, just as do ordinary men. Because Byron wrote, "Let *he* who made thee answer that," it does not follow that we are to use the nominative case of the pronoun with the imperative of the third person. All that it shows is that Byron was not correct in his grammar. The Dean pleads custom. Custom is undoubtedly high authority. We are all familiar with the dictum of Horace,

Si volet usus,
Quem penes arbitrium est, et jus, et norma loquendi.

But the custom of whom do we accept as the standard? Of children? of the ignorant and uncultivated? Or does the voice even of the majority of those who are educated determine grammatical rules? Or is it the usage of the best writers and speakers? Really it seems almost childish to ask these questions. But the persistence of the Dean and his followers renders it necessary to go back to the very elements. "For when "for the time ye ought to be teachers, ye have need that "one teach you again which are the first principles." The laws of grammar are not the work of pedants and fools, as some would have us believe, but inductions rigorously made from the facts presented by an examination of the language.

Hear the conclusion of the whole matter. We should correct our own mistakes if we are to instruct others with authority; we are not to be a law unto ourselves, rejecting those general laws of language which have been established for ages, and pleading the custom and usage of the unlettered many, against the example and practice of the cultivated few, but we are to accept those things as fixed, which the most diligent students of the language have discovered to be the normal and prevalent modes of expression. If any sneer at grammarians and their rules, a greater than the scoffers thus spoke: "Whoever in a state knows how to form wisely the "manners of men and to rule them at home and in war, "by excellent institutes, him in the first place, above "others, I should esteem worthy of all honour; but next "to him the man who strives to establish in maxims and "rules the method and habit of speaking and writing "derived from a good age of the nation, and, as it were, "to fortify the same round with a kind of wall, the daring "to overleap which, a law, only short of that of Romulus, "should be used to prevent."* Thus wrote John Milton.

THE DEAN'S ENGLISH.

A Criticism from 'The Phonetic Journal.'

If, as some good people hold, everybody and everything is created, not merely for a general, but moreover for some specific, purpose, then we might infer that the particular use to which Nature destined the Dean of Canterbury was to set himself up to lecture upon the Queen's English, and so, to offer himself as a conspicuous mark, and a defenceless victim, to the scathing criticism and merciless exposure of Mr. G. Washington Moon. Not for many

* The Dean's English, p. 94.

years, have we seen such a brilliant and effective passage of arms, as is contained in the little book under notice, which consists principally of three letters addressed to Dr. Alford. To say, that the poor Dean is worsted in the encounter, is to say very little. His defeat is almost too complete. Like an untrained youth, in the grasp of an athlete, he never has even a chance. At every round, he is quickly thrown; and the blows, given with a will, and planted with a precision and vigour, which no feint can elude, fall fast and heavily on his defenceless head. At every point, the Dean is confronted by his pertinacious and inexorable assailant, who leaves him no possibility of escape; or, if he does occasionally attempt a feeble defence, it serves only to bring down upon himself still severer punishment, until, exhausted by the encounter, he does that, which, for his own sake, he had better have done at first—makes peace with his adversary while yet he is in the way with him.

To set up one's self for a teacher of English, pure and undefiled; jauntily to ascend the rostrum, as one gifted with authority to lay down the whole law; and then to be met with such a withering exposure of incompetence, with such inevitable inferences of imbecility, as constitute the staple of Mr. Moon's book; for the physician, who gratuitously obtrudes his advice upon us, and vaunts his ability to cure our disorder,—for him to be convicted of labouring under a virulent form of the same disease, certainly this is *not* a pleasant position for a man to occupy, and we heartily commiserate the unfortunate Dean.

Even in the fair field of criticism he is quite unable to cope with his skilful and alert adversary. Never was there a more conspicuous instance of going out to shear, and coming home shorn. For our own part we would rather have submitted to a month's stone-breaking than have called down upon ourselves such withering sarcasms and incisive irony as Dr. Alford's language has so justly provoked.

To those who are interested in speaking and writing good English,—and what educated person is not?—this book is full of instruction; and to those who enjoy a controversy, conducted with consummate skill, and in excellent taste by a strong man, well armed, it is such a treat as does not fall in one's way often during a life-time. Regarded in itself, and without any immediate reference to its object, this book affords a model of correct and elegant English; such as is a perfect treat to meet with, in these days of slip-shod writing. Perspicuous, compact and nervous in its construction, it is by no means deficient in some of the higher and more brilliant qualities of style; while, for refined sarcasm and covert irony, it has rarely been equalled. We can assure our readers that a pleasanter or more profitable employment than the perusal of this book, it would be difficult to recommend to them. As the subject is not of an ephemeral nature, though the book itself was called forth by a passing occasion, we hope to see the public interest in the work wax, rather than wane, and that still more editions may yet be called for. Every copy that is circulated is so much good seed sown broadcast,—so much seed of tares smothered in its growth.

Many of our public writers, highly educated, and perhaps *because* they have been so educated, undertake English composition as if it were the one exceptional art which requires no rule but the "rule of thumb." To such, the lamentable *fiasco* of the Dean, owing to his disregard of rules *should* be a lesson, but, too probably, will not. We cannot help wishing that a writer who is so eminently qualified as Mr. Moon to teach a subject which, just now, so greatly needs to be taught, and who illustrates so admirably by his example the precepts which he so clearly enforces, would devote himself to the task of drawing up a code of rules for composition, such as our journalists might appeal to, as a standard for correct English. We are of opinion that there is a crying want of such a work, that it would be one of the most useful and most popular works of the day, and that Mr. Moon, with his thorough mastery of the subject, is just the person to write it.

Students of the Language are recommended to procure

THE COMPANION VOLUME,

Price 3s. 6d.

ENTITLED

BAD ENGLISH EXPOSED:

A Series of Criticisms

ON THE ERRORS AND INCONSISTENCIES OF

LINDLEY MURRAY AND OTHER GRAMMARIANS.

FITFH EDITION.

BY

G. WASHINGTON MOON, F.R.S.L.

Author of 'The Devn's English'

LONDON: HATCHARDS, 187 PICCADILLY.

BY THE SAME AUTHOR.

BAD ENGLISH EXPOSED.

FIFTH EDITION.

Price 3s. 6d.

EXTRACTS FROM REVIEWS.

Mr. Moon points out many real inaccuracies of language.—THE SATURDAY REVIEW.

This work is well worthy of the careful study of all who aspire to write English elegantly and accurately.—THE LONDON QUARTERLY REVIEW.

We commend the work to the attention of all those who are interested in preserving the purity of the English tongue.—THE FRIEND.

We heartily recommend the work to students, as containing many valuable instructions for those who desire to attain a thorough knowledge of the art of English composition.—THE MORNING POST.

Like the author's now celebrated 'Dean's English,' it is characterised by vivacity of style and a complete mastery of the niceties of our mother tongue.—THE EDUCATIONAL RECORD.

There is something very inviting in the work of a man who, having fairly unhorsed the Dean of Canterbury in his own chosen lists, has now the audacity to attack the great arbiter of such contests, Lindley Murray himself.

We confess our obligation to Mr. Moon, not only for an instructive but for an entertaining book; and we believe that there are few who do not often fall into errors which he condemns, or who cannot learn from him, in a very pleasant way, to write and to speak English more elegantly.—THE NEW YORK CHURCH RECORD.

Mr. Moon probably attains the extremest point of invulnerability. The elegance and accuracy of his style are so extraordinary as to be almost unique.—THE NEW YORK ROUND TABLE.

The book is a splendid specimen of what a controversial work should be—keen, incisive, vigorous, yet discriminating and perfectly courteous. It will be a valuable work for purposes of reference and guidance long after the memory of the controversy which excited it has faded away.—THE COURT CIRCULAR.

The English language is a noble inheritance, and we may well be thankful to those who, like Mr. Moon, jealously guard its purity. There are, indeed, but few, either readers or writers of the English language, who do not need to profit by his very instructive criticisms.—THE QUARTERLY JOURNAL OF EDUCATION.

Mr. Washington Moon writes with considerable elegance and remarkable perspicuity. His book is both amusing and instructive, and may be read with advantage by all who wish to acquire a correct mode of writing and speaking, and to avoid the popular errors which are in some danger of being permanently incorporated into our language.—THE INQUIRER.

The volume abounds with the clear and keen criticisms of one who has every right to speak with very high authority. It redounds to the credit not only of Mr. Moon, but to the credit of our English literature. It is a work that ought by all means to find its way into the hands of our best schoolmasters and their pupils, and all scholars and students of our language.—THE ROCK.

Mr. Moon is a chivalrous opponent, ready with hearty goodwill to espouse the cause of a former adversary when unjustly attacked, as may be seen in his defence of Dean Alford against the strictures of Mr. Gould. Those who desire to express their ideas clearly and grammatically can hardly fail to benefit by a perusal of Mr. Moon's essays, although they may not acquire his power of acute criticism, nor his mastery over the English language.—THE RECORD.

BAD ENGLISH EXPOSED.

Mr. Moon has produced another series of witticisms at the expense of sundry distinguished men who have made the grammar and history of the English language their study. The volume is very instructive and highly amusing; and if the author betrays some ostentatious triumph, he does this with admirable temper.—THE BRITISH QUARTERLY REVIEW.

In Mr. Moon's hands, a subject universally dry and dull becomes most amusing. His style is clear and trenchant: he deals firmly and at the same time good-humouredly with his opponents. In exposing some of the common grammatical errors of our language to-day—errors which custom has now familiarized—he has rendered a great service to Englishmen, and deserves our warmest commendation.—LLOYD'S WEEKLY NEWS.

The English language has not often been thoroughly mastered, and there have been few at any time who have been able to use it with correctness and taste. A distinguished scholar of the eighteenth century said that in his lifetime he had known only three men who spoke their native language with uniform grammatical accuracy. Mr. Moon has obviously studied with great diligence the rules of English construction, by no means easy to master. The book is very valuable and very important. We unhesitatingly commend it.—THE SUNDAY TIMES.

Mr. Washington Moon is now no stranger to the public. He has laid before it two series of literary productions, so diverse from each other in character, that future generations will be tempted to believe there must have been, in the nineteenth century, two authors of the name of Washington Moon, whose works somehow became confounded together. Gaining the reputation of a severe critic by a determined onslaught which he made on a composition of Dean Alford's, he next launched an epic poem, 'Elijah,' containing many a glorious stanza.

The work now under review will fully sustain Mr. Moon's high reputation. As a critic able and accurate, we have an unbounded respect for our author.—THE WEEKLY REVIEW.

LONDON: HATCHARDS, PICCADILLY.

BY THE SAME AUTHOR.

ELIJAH THE PROPHET:
A POEM.
THIRD EDITION.
Price 3s. 6d.

EXTRACTS FROM REVIEWS.

It is an epic poem of great beauty and power.—THE WEEKLY RECORD.

An epic poem containing many a glorious stanza.—THE WEEKLY REVIEW.

It is really a sacred epic of the highest order.—THE ORB.

This is a remarkable poem, and is from first to last worthy of its subject.—OUR OWN FIRESIDE.

It is a poem worthy of the subject and of the author.—THE CHRISTIAN EXAMINER.

'Elijah the Prophet' is the most noticeable poem of the season. It is poetical in the true sense of the term.—THE BOOKSELLER.

It is full of quiet beauty, and is specially remarkable for elegance of diction and purity of language.—THE FREEMAN.

We are bound to remark that, taken as a whole, it is by far the best poem on a sacred subject that has appeared for a considerable time.—THE IMPERIAL REVIEW.

This poem is one of unusual interest and beauty. It will find favour chiefly with persons of refined and cultivated taste, who can appreciate the nicer elegancies of composition.—EVANGELICAL CHRISTENDOM.

The magnificent epic poem before us is one of those rare issues, which, like wandering comets, appear only at long intervals. Every page teems with high poetic beauties, often soaring to the sublime.—THE ILLUSTRATED WEEKLY NEWS.

In this work the library has one of the most valuable additions that have for many years emanated from the press. Gifted with a master-mind,—imaginative, penetrative, refined, and modest withal,—the author of this poem has thrown the full force of his powers of expression into the accomplishment of a great end, namely, the effective rendering, with the aid of poetry, of one of the most sublime records in the Old Testament.—THE OXFORD UNIVERSITY HERALD.

The author has not only the attributes and qualifications of a poet in the true and highest sense, but a rare amount of varied knowledge, which he brings in the happiest manner to bear on the grand heads of his subject. We have not for many a day perused a volume of poetry that possesses so many attractive features. The book is one series of beautiful and brilliant gems and profound thoughts, set in pure and ornate language.—St. James's Chronicle.

It is awarding no slight merit to the author to say that his whole poem breathes the purest morality and the loftiest devotion. Going through it is like going through a cathedral, where, as the grand music rolls on the ear, the eye is almost everywhere enchanted with visions of unearthly interest and scriptural beauty breaking in richest colour from its storied windows, while the soul is touched and stirred with the deepest emotions of religion.—The Church Gazette.

BY THE SAME AUTHOR.

One volume, uniform with 'Elijah the Prophet.'

EDEN THE GARDEN OF GOD,
AND OTHER POEMS.
THIRD EDITION.
Price 3s. 6d.

EXTRACTS FROM REVIEWS.

The volume only needs to be known to become a favourite.—The Freeman.

The poetry is really chaste and beautiful.—Evangelical Christendom.

We recommend this volume of genuine poetry as one of the best gift-books of the season.—Our Own Fireside.

Mr. Washington Moon knows the secrets of both the strength and the grace of his own tongue.—The London Quarterly Review.

Mr. Washington Moon's minor poems have deservedly reached a second edition; some of them being of great beauty.—The John Bull.

Mr. Washington Moon's minor poems have a polished beauty and earnestness of feeling which will secure for some among them a lasting place in English sacred poetry. They are of elevated morality, of fervent devotion, and of fascinating eloquence in song.—St. James's Chronicle.

THE COMPANION VOLUME TO THE 'SOUL'S INQUIRIES.'

Price 1s. 6d. cloth; 2s. 6d. roan, gilt edges.

THE SOUL'S DESIRES

BREATHED TO GOD
IN THE WORDS OF SCRIPTURE.

A Book of Prayers for Private and Family Devotion.

TO WHICH IS PREFIXED,

WHAT THE BIBLE SAYS ABOUT PRAYER.

SECOND THOUSAND.

HATCHARDS, PUBLISHERS, 187 PICCADILLY, LONDON.

ALSO BY THE SAME AUTHOR.

Price 2s. 6d. cloth; 3s. 6d. roan, gilt edges.

THE SOUL'S COMFORT IN SORROW.

"When I would comfort myself against sorrow, my heart is faint in me."—JER. viii. 18.

"Faint not when the dark sky lowers,
 And all seemeth gloom above;
For 'tis then refreshing showers
Come to cheer the drooping flowers,
 And these teach us 'GOD is love.'"—P. 61.

SELECTIONS

FROM

"𝕲𝖔𝖉'𝖘 𝖊𝖝𝖈𝖊𝖊𝖉𝖎𝖓𝖌 𝕲𝖗𝖊𝖆𝖙 𝖆𝖓𝖉 𝕻𝖗𝖊𝖈𝖎𝖔𝖚𝖘 𝕻𝖗𝖔𝖒𝖎𝖘𝖊𝖘,"

AND FROM THE POETICAL WRITINGS OF

G. WASHINGTON MOON, F.R.S.L.

Author of "The Soul's Desires Breathed to God."
"The Soul's Inquiries Answered in the Words of Scripture," &c.

HATCHARDS, PUBLISHERS, 187 PICCADILLY, LONDON.

BY THE SAME AUTHOR.

UNIFORM WITH THE PREVIOUS WORK.

Price 2s. 6d. cloth antique; 3s. 6d. roan, gilt edges.
(*Cheaper Edition,* 1s. 6d.)

THE SOUL'S INQUIRIES
ANSWERED IN THE WORDS OF SCRIPTURE:

"As if a man had inquired at the Oracle of God."—
2 SAMUEL, xvi, 23.

"Call THOU and I will answer; or let me speak, and answer THOU me."—JOB, xiii, 22.

A Year-Book of Scripture Texts.

THIRTEENTH THOUSAND.

EXTRACTS FROM REVIEWS.

We cordially recommend this book.—THE CHRISTIAN AMBASSADOR.

It is calculated to do immense good.—THE HOME JOURNAL (PHILADELPHIA, U.S.A.).

It is a Scripture text-book of unequalled excellence.—THE GENERAL BAPTIST MAGAZINE.

It is the most attractive and useful work of the kind we have yet seen.—THE SUNDAY-SCHOOL TEACHER.

We can have no hesitation in recommending it to favourable notice.—THE BRITISH FRIEND.

We trust that to many a pilgrim-heart it will be a blessed companion.—THE ADVENT HERALD (BOSTON, U.S.A.).

It is an exceedingly valuable little book which many devout persons will, we think, be glad to possess.—THE CHRISTIAN OBSERVER.

It is a compilation of rare excellence, very far superior to any other book of the kind we have seen.—The Presbyterian Witness (Halifax, N. S.).

It is the best birthday text-book we have seen. Most instructive, suggestive, striking, valuable. Far better than anything of the kind before in print.—The Sword and Trowel.

The striking way in which the grand doctrines of Christianity are set forth one after another must make this pretty little work much valued.—The Daily Witness (Montreal).

A happy idea happily carried out. All the great questions which man can ask about God and Christ and himself, the life that now is, and the life to come, are here asked and answered in Scripture language.—The Freeman.

What could be happier than the thought to arrange a diary in such a manner that, open it where we may, we light upon some divine words of counsel or of comfort, borrowed from the Sacred Oracles? This year-book of Scripture texts ought to win the widest popularity.—The St. James's Chronicle.

It would not be a difficult task for any person of ordinary mental power to commit to memory, day by day, all the questions and answers in this book; by doing which he would, in a year, have possessed himself of a rich treasury of Scripture truth that would afford unfailing light, strength, and consolation in all the varied circumstances of life.—The Christian Guardian (Toronto).

Among selections of texts for daily reading and meditation we have seen few equal to this. Every word of God is good and helpful to the soul, but this book contains the result of much profound Scripture study, and is at once a mine of rich theology and a manual of practical piety. It is most valuable, and should be heartily welcomed in Christian homes.—The Scottish Sabbath-School Teachers' Magazine.

London: HATCHARDS, Piccadilly.

www.ingramcontent.com/pod-product-compliance
Lightning Source LLC
Chambersburg PA
CBHW031743230426
43669CB00007B/453